The Failure of
Environmental Education (And
How We Can Fix It)

The Failure of Environmental Education (And How We Can Fix It)

Charles Saylan and Daniel T. Blumstein

UNIVERSITY OF CALIFORNIA PRESS

Berkeley   Los Angeles   London

University of California Press, one of the most distinguished university presses in the United States, enriches
lives around the world by advancing scholarship in the
humanities, social sciences, and natural sciences. Its activities are supported by the UC Press Foundation and by
philanthropic contributions from individuals and institutions. For more information, visit www.ucpress.edu.

University of California Press
Berkeley and Los Angeles, California

University of California Press, Ltd.
London, England

Library of Congress Cataloging-in-Publication Data

Saylan, Charles, 1953–.
    The failure of environmental education (and how we
can fix it) / Charles Saylan and Daniel T. Blumstein.
        p.   cm.
    Includes bibliographical references and index.
    ISBN 978-0-520-26538-7 (cloth : alk. paper)—ISBN
978-0-520-26539-4 (pbk. : alk. paper)
    1. Environmental education.   I. Blumstein, Daniel
T.   II. Title.
    GE70.S29   2011
    333.7071—dc22   2010040205

Manufactured in the United States of America

20 19 18 17 16 15 14 13 12 11
10 9 8 7 6 5 4 3 2 1

This book is printed on Cascades Enviro 100, a 100% post
consumer waste, recycled, de-inked fiber. FSC recycled
certified and processed chlorine free. It is acid free,
Ecologo certified, and manufactured by BioGas energy.

Charlie: For Maddalena, with love, and Burbank,
with tennis ball

Dan: To David and Janice, my partners in
exploration and discovery

CONTENTS

PREFACE

There are noticeably fewer places these days where one can experience the immensity of nature, where one can feel alone and far from the societal order that humanity seems driven to impose on the random wilderness. It is harder to hear the wind howl across some distant ridge, as trees are fewer now, felled by ever-expanding and efficient industry. Not long ago, within the scope of the authors' personal memories, one might have ventured into the wilderness and found no trace of humans. Today, however, humanity's footprint is almost everywhere. Out in the woods are anonymous fences that mask the grand exfoliation of mining, hydroelectric plants, or oil pipelines. Gazing up from almost anywhere, one sees jet contrails filling the sky with the graffiti of human presence. Looking deeper into the natural world reveals changes in animal behavior and ecology caused by the long arm of anthropogenic effects, like the presence of human toxins in the fat of top predators that live in remote places where humans are never encountered. Even the wilderness areas our governments set aside for protection have diminished over the years under the prevailing belief that growth and development are synonymous with success.

From childhood, we each had the privilege of experiencing the freedom that roaming the wilderness offers, as hikers and mountaineers, as skiers and sailors, as biologists and teachers. That freedom sowed in us the seed of a profound respect for and love of nature. Our concept of nature was as immense as the outdoors, as vast as the horizon, as deep as outer space.

When we were young, we were taught that the population of our planet was just under three billion, a number that seemed incomprehensibly large to a fourth grader. In significantly less than a lifetime, however, the population has more than doubled and may soon double again. Sadly, the space we enjoyed as children is shrinking, and the wild unexplored places that inspired us so deeply are now mostly gone.

We have witnessed growth unprecedented in the history of our species and our planet, initially with a sense of pride and wonder at technologies that seemed like something out of science fiction. But as these advances became real and accessible, our wonder became clouded with uncomfortable foreboding. The irrepressible nature we enjoyed and had taken for granted seemed increasingly threatened by unlikely sources that, just a few years earlier, were touted as the cutting edge of humankind's progress. Industry, development, better living, travel, and consumerism, to name a few, started revealing their unforeseen ramifications. Nobody's fault, really. Something, we hoped, that could be addressed by focusing human ingenuity on the problems. After all, we all have an unwavering faith in our collective ability to solve problems by applying technology. Right?

But as time passed and we looked deeper into these issues, we found they were not just isolated problems easily corrected. We slowly began to believe that what was being uncovered was only the tip of an immense iceberg, the magnitude of which humanity still does not comprehend. And our faith in human ingenuity was confused and shaken. It was that very same ingenuity, for the most part, that brought about this assault on nature.

We are both fortunate to have grown up with abundant opportunity to experience the wilderness in many forms, and we care deeply and personally that the opportunities we enjoyed will not be lost to children of future generations. Our children. Your children. Nature is a humbling force that teaches us we are all part of a greater system. Whether one chooses to believe that the origins of such complexity are random or divine is unimportant. Nature, a very different nature, will persist as some new balance sorts itself out. Evolution will proceed. It is humanity's place in the balance that is threatened.

Our perspective emerges from a combination of our two diverse backgrounds: Blumstein as scientist and educator, and Saylan as entrepreneur and, later, director of an environmental nonprofit. This diversity helps us approach this subject in a novel way. Each of us has worked toward raising public awareness of environmental issues in different ways. We have written popular articles, given public talks, and designed and implemented educational programs, albeit on a relatively small scale. We have repeatedly followed available funding, sometimes reformatting our programs to fit grantor's parameters and carefully wording our evaluations of program effectiveness in ways that would not jeopardize future opportunities by seeming negative. From very different experiences, and for very different reasons, we both arrived at the stark conclusion that both environmental education in its current state, and the institutions responsible for its implementation, do not effectively provide what is necessary to turn the tide of environmental deterioration. Importantly, we believe that this failing has not been widely recognized.

We firmly believe that change is not only possible but within reach if all of us begin to look at the problems differently and accept the collective and individual responsibilities required for wise stewardship of our earth. This, however, is no easy task. We hope future generations will have fish to eat, unpolluted water to drink, and a rich web of vibrant ecosystem services. We hope future generations will hike, bike, sail, and explore and enjoy what we so enjoyed growing up: open spaces, biodiversity, nature's processes. We hope this book helps achieve this vision.

CHAPTER ONE

The Problem(s)

Environmental education has failed to bring about the changes in attitude and behavior necessary to stave off the detrimental effects of climate change, biodiversity loss, and environmental degradation that our planet is experiencing at an alarmingly accelerating rate.

For decades, scientists have warned of the potentially devastating consequences of climate change, and although it has become a highly politicized issue, serious problems still loom in earth's near future. A conservative approach would dictate that our societies act expediently to mitigate these potential threats. But that is not happening. Instead, we are all paralyzed by indecision, argument, misplaced politicization of the issues, and a widespread lack of commitment to change. The pace of environmental degradation, however, is not slowing.

This collective inability to act is brought about in part by educational institutions that generally do not provide the tools necessary for critical thinking and for understanding the modern world. Nor do they teach individual responsibility and social engagement, two fundamental tenets of free and democratic societies.

So what exactly is it that is failing? Is it environmental education or education as a whole? We believe they may, in fact, be one and the same. Although many consider environmental education to be a subheading of science education, it must be more than that. Not only must environmental education teach people about their physical environment, it must go further to teach how to live and flourish in sustainable ways. Environmental education has failed in part because of its limitations.

Who can be held responsible for this inefficacy? In fairness, the blame must be borne by everyone, as we are all responsible citizens of earth, whether or not we choose to acknowledge it. Each of us bears a moral responsibility to protect the resources that support life on our planet, not only for those we share the planet with, but also for those who will come after us. If our societies fail to do this, they fail humanity. People have the collective power to effect change on local and national levels alike. But that power must be realized and acted on by individuals, and we believe that education has a role in providing the skills to do so.

As parents, we must work to assure a safe and healthy future for our children. A future that includes time spent exploring wild places and learning about the creatures that inhabit them. A future that helps children learn who they are by connecting them to where they live.

As teachers, we should work toward providing students with the creative and analytical skills they will need to live good lives within whatever communities they choose. We should also strive to instill a creative curiosity about the world and an interest in learning that will remain with students throughout their lives. Just as important, we need to stay focused on improving the institutions in which we teach and our personal skills and abilities as well.

As students, we must hunger for more exposure to new and broader concepts. We must understand that we are authors of the future of our communities and nations, and that we possess the power to make ourselves heard and to effect change.

And as policy makers, we must listen carefully for the voice of the people and encourage participatory good citizenry at every opportunity.

What is needed is a modern, practical redefinition of environmental education. One that encompasses multidisciplinary teaching approaches. One that seeks to cultivate scientific and civic literacy. One that stimulates community engagement, fosters an understanding of moral systems, and reinforces the appreciation of aesthetics. We believe it is time for a full integration of environmental education in a form that inspires practical and critical reevaluation of education as a whole. We believe this reevaluation will lead to synergistic action and real impact.

The obstacles to such an educational approach are many and diverse. Understanding the complexity of the environmental problems facing our world requires a working knowledge of politics, consumption, the nature and state of educational and legislative institutions, effective metrics for measuring successes and failures, and a healthy dose of background information. Together, these ideas and disciplines will create a new vision of environmental education and environmental literacy.

Our societies increasingly seem to hunger for information in the form of distilled snippets and simple solutions, quickly expressed and easily digested. Perhaps, because of the barrage of information that confronts us all daily, the trend seems to be toward a synoptic world of bullet points and "elevator speeches." But the problems affecting education, and consequently society, are too diverse to be assimilated quickly. If the solutions were simple, the problems would have been solved by now, and this book would not be necessary.

The arguments we will develop require some short-term faith on the part of the reader. We will, at times, go against the typical definitions and responsibilities of education. We may sometimes sound utopian as we offer diverse ideas on our duties as parents, educators, scientists, and citizens. Nevertheless, we strongly believe these things must be said and that a new approach for environmental education must emerge. We believe a comprehensive, integrated, revitalized, and revised environmental education is essential for the survival of us all.

We hope that humanity will flourish in increasing harmony with its surroundings. Humans are creatures of remarkable capacity and, without question, have the ability to find a sustainable place in this world. People need only the collective will to do it. So, how can this metamorphosis come about? We think environmental education is a logical and essential step in the process. But we must qualify this statement by emphasizing that the education of which we speak must be responsive, self-critical, flexible, and focused on the common goal of immediately reducing our destructive human impact on the ecological systems that support us.

We want to provide a sort of manifesto for addressing how people think about environmental education, rather than a fix-it list for troubled, politicized, and overly bureaucratic educational systems. But to do that, we'll need to look deeper into those educational systems and the political climates in which many exist. Readers need to understand why education is not providing the tools and skills that people need in order to mitigate or circumvent the grave environmental problems our societies now face.

Has environmental education really failed? Imagine a graph on which the horizontal axis represents all the effort and resources expended toward making the public aware of the degradation of the environment, and the vertical axis represents the progress of the degradation itself. It would be great if efforts tended to decrease degradation, such that the line on the graph sloped down and to the right. We do not believe that is happening. This is not to say that there has not been tremendous public awareness derived from the efforts to date. Without environmental education, the planet would likely be in an even bigger, more incomprehensible mess. Even so, we believe environmental education is simply not effective enough or sufficiently available to change individual and collective behavior enough to affect the problems at hand. And we are firmly convinced that time is running out.

The problems with education are systemic, and we aim to offer a new perspective and synthesis to people at all levels of the educational process: teachers, parents, students, administrators, and those who make public policy. We hope that the "people in the trenches"—the educators our societies rely on to teach responsible stewardship—will find our ideas useful in shaping their own approach to an uncertain future. They make up a talented, passionate, and committed group of people, many of whom have been the groundbreakers for helping to establish the levels of public awareness that make a book like this one possible.

In writing this book we wished to put forth a positive and proactive message. There is increasing sentiment both within and outside the environmental-education community that taking a "doom and gloom" approach turns people off to any message that actions can make positive impacts on the world around us. Perhaps there is some truth to that, and we attempt herein to frame our argument in terms we hope will inspire thought and action, rather than leaving readers feeling helpless and overwhelmed.

There are, however, some emerging discoveries and data about the problems we are likely to face in the near future that warrant elucidation. They are neither pleasant nor positive. Yet they set the context in which we write this book, and we believe that readers must understand what the world may look like if humanity continues its business as usual. This realization should help readers understand why we believe environmental education, as it presently stands, does not serve the purposes for which it is intended, and that this is a most urgent matter worthy of collective attention.

There is little doubt our planet is getting warmer. In its most recent report, released in 2007, the Nobel Prize–winning Intergovernmental Panel on Climate Change (IPCC) wrote that "warming of the climate system is unequivocal," and, quite notably, that "most of the observed increase in global average temperatures since the mid-20th century is very likely due to the observed increase in anthropogenic greenhouse gas concentrations."[1] Greenhouse gasses are not new, but the biophysical and geochemical cycles that regulate them have been affected by how energy has been used since the dawn of the industrial revolution. Burning fossil fuels releases carbon from the earth into the atmosphere, and the sum total of these anthropogenic sources is heating the earth's atmosphere. How much? How fast? That is what the IPCC seeks to understand.

The IPCC is an organization made up of contributors from 130 countries that work under strict consensus. This means that any country has veto power over statements and conclusions made in the final report. Stop and think about that for a moment.

Take, for example, a major industrial country that doesn't like an interpretation of the rate at which polar sea ice is melting because it might contribute to actions that spark national unemployment if profitable but "dirty" industries are cleaned up, or are cleaned up too quickly. Or, consider a rapidly developing country that views the prediction of sea level rise tied directly to greenhouse gas emissions as a threat to the development that is helping reduce poverty and disease and increase longevity within its borders. Either, or both, of these countries' IPCC representatives might veto a strong environmental statement in favor of a statement of milder predictions that will have less of an economic impact in its respective country. Practically speaking, that means the IPCC consensus report is a *very* conservative estimate of the likely consequences of rising atmospheric greenhouse gasses. And even in its "watered down" consensus form, it's a truly frightening read.

In the 2006 documentary *An Inconvenient Truth*, former U.S. vice president Al Gore explained the mechanics of greenhouse gas emissions for a popular audience. It became the fourth-highest-grossing U.S. documentary film of all time. The film helped lift the veil of misinformation surrounding global warming issues perpetrated on the public by political naysayers and special interest lobbyists. It also brought new acceptance and discussion of the problems associated with climate change into the international limelight.

Another important milestone was the publication in 2006 of *The Economics of Climate Change* by the eminent British economist Lord Nicholas Stern. The report focused on the assessment of future impacts of global warming on world economies. Essentially, the report states that the benefits of concise and early action, on the part of world governments, to reduce the effects of global warming far outweigh the costs. Lord Stern went on to say that an immediate and continued investment of 1 percent per annum of the global gross domestic product (GDP) is necessary to offset the worst effects of climate change, which include a "major disruption of economic and social activities" on a scale that could rival the effects of both world wars or the Great Depression.[2] In 2008, Stern emended his recommendation to a 2 percent investment of GDP, based on data that showed global warming trends were increasing at levels greater than previously estimated.[3]

As a result of increasing media coverage, we all know that carbon dioxide emissions are a major cause of climate change. We also know that these emissions, despite years of negotiations and discussion by the world's nations about how to reduce their release, are still increasing, not decreasing. Although there is still a good amount of debate and discussion as to how much is too much and whether and where the tipping points—that is, the atmospheric CO_2 levels beyond which there will be massive and irreversible changes in the global temperature—might be, considerable effort is being expended to find new sources of sustainable energy, ways to reduce automobile and industrial emissions, and scenarios by which carbon emissions can be capped and traded commercially. These are positive steps, but because they are based on a consensus view that is intrinsically biased toward underestimating the severity of the problem, they are just not enough.

Indeed, if one believes the political rhetoric and mainstream media, it might seem we have turned the corner on global warming and are taking the necessary steps to mitigate its effects. This is especially true if one holds an unshakeable faith in human ingenuity or subscribes to the "humanity can fix anything with technology" school. Despite increased public awareness, most people still believe the effects of climate change will appear sometime in the vague future, when in actuality the effects are visible today. It seems when things deteriorate gradually, people tend not to notice them. The image of shifting baselines is a compelling one: a little change here, a little change there, and it all starts to seem normal. Thus, people do not see the potential for catastrophe unless something dramatic and immediate occurs. In the time frame of global warming issues, it would probably be too late to do much about the effects or causes of such an event.

The major public focus has been on industrial carbon emissions and sources of efficient energy, but some other serious issues associated with climate change require attention as well. Scientists are learning more every day, and some of what we have been reading in the primary scientific literature indicates potential negative impacts of a magnitude far greater than previously thought.

There has been widespread discussion of melting polar ice and what effects it might have on our world. The effects discussed range from the loss of polar bear habitats to potential economic benefits of new, less costly shipping routes, but there is more. In May 2008, researchers from the University of California at Riverside and Flinders University in Australia published findings revealing a relatively sudden release of methane, a greenhouse gas some twenty-three times more potent than CO_2. This release occurred 635 million years ago, causing an abrupt shift in planetary climate from the stable "snowball" ice age to a much warmer, stable state, with little time in between.[4] The study shows how methane was initially released gradually through destabilization of ice sheets, which, as they melted, released pressure on clathrates—a form of methane ice held stable by temperature and pressure—triggering substantially increased levels of the gas. Clathrates remain present today in their dormant state, both in arctic permafrost and in sediments on the ocean floor. The concern here is that small increases in global temperatures, such as those we are currently experiencing as a consequence of our widespread addiction to oil and coal, may trigger a similar release of methane gas. One scenario by which this could happen would result from the polar regions absorbing more heat if the reflective snow melts sooner each year both over the arctic tundra and the Arctic and Antarctic oceans. Snow and ice, because they are white, reflect light and therefore heat. This reflectance is lost when the snow and ice melt and resulting darker earth and water surfaces absorb the sun's energy as heat. Thus, permafrost, which contains frozen methane, would melt and clathrates would release their methane. The ramifications of these events, which could happen very quickly, would be catastrophic and are thought to be irreversible.[5] The resulting substantial increase in methane outgassing could overshadow all benefits gained from current attempts to reduce anthropogenic carbon emissions.

If current estimates are correct for methane release from permafrost, some 100 billion tons could be released into our atmosphere this century. That's a huge number. If one assumes an adult elephant weighs five thousand kilograms, then that's like putting twenty billion elephants into the atmosphere, or 556 million blue whales, or 3.8 million Titanics. One hundred billion tons of methane is 333 times the total mass of humans on earth. Should this catastrophe occur, earth could experience climate warming that is equivalent to 270 years of emissions at today's levels.

Another, more controversial effect of melting polar ice is the resulting change in ocean salinity that could lead to a slowing or stoppage of the thermohaline circulation. This is an oceanographic mechanism whereby warm water from the tropics is carried northward via surface wind-driven currents like the Gulf Stream. As the water moves toward the polar region, it cools and its density increases. This denser water consequently sinks into deep ocean basins, where it moves southward within these basins to resurface again as it is heated. Such upwelling is a source of considerable nutrient cycling in the oceans, and this "ocean conveyor belt" is, in part, responsible for the stability of earth's weather patterns. As freshwater from melting ice enters the oceans in vast quantity, the salinity, and consequently the density, of seawater will change, potentially causing the thermohaline circulation to slow or stop. Speculation on the specific effects of such an occurrence include outcomes ranging from moderate changes in the productivity and climate of Europe, to radical alterations in global weather patterns. Such changes could, among other things, significantly reduce rainfall levels from the Asian monsoon, on which a third of the world's population depends for irrigation of agricultural crops.[6]

Seawater becomes acidified when CO_2 from fossil-fuel combustion and other sources is absorbed from the atmosphere by ocean waters. This creates carbonic acid, which increases the acidity of the oceans from their natural, basic state. If the pH level is too low, calcium carbonate cannot be formed. Since the onset of industrialization, ocean acidification has increased 30 percent, which completely overwhelms any natural mechanisms that might counteract this phenomenon. This process is further exacerbated by deforestation, which is increasing globally as well. Recent research has shown that the time frame for ocean acidification is accelerating, and detrimental effects may emerge in decades, rather than centuries as previously thought.[7] A more acidic ocean could, among other things, drive phytoplankton extinct. Under this scenario, not only would the ocean cease to remove carbon from the atmosphere, but there would be no food for fish to eat, and no fish for us to eat. This could threaten global food security and create severe economic impacts, especially in areas that depend on the sea for sustenance. Coral reefs, already threatened, may essentially vanish from most areas by midcentury, leaving coastal communities open to erosion and flooding, causing a further loss of fish habitat and creating economic damages in the billions. Perhaps the start of this will be a more acidic ocean, in which the ecosystems and ecosystem services that we depend on fail to thrive, producers of slime and toxic algal blooms are quite at home, and hypoxia and dead zones abound. Should this come to pass, it will likely happen in the next hundred or so years, but it will take thousands of years to recover to a state that even resembles what we know today.

Other resource management issues, such as overfishing, have little to do with global warming directly but, in the coming decades, will likely have major negative effects on our well-being. Where ocean acidification tends to attack the ecosystem from the bottom up, overfishing tends to work from the top down.

Historically, ocean fisheries have been regarded as infinite resources, able to provide a growing population with everlasting food, fertilizers, and medicines, among other things. To understand why this is so, one need only stand on the beach and look seaward. As one confronts the vastness of the ocean's horizon, the idea that our populations are capable of taking everything useful out of the sea seems ridiculous, arrogant, and impossible. But the reality is otherwise, and humanity is well on its way toward taking far more than the oceans can ever replace. Recent studies indicate that we humans have fished our way to the point where one-third of available stocks are depleted, and we're all proceeding down the food chain with alarming speed. Scientists speculate that unless fisheries management policies are not changed radically and soon, this is the last century in which people will enjoy wild seafood.[8]

Aside from the 50 billion or so dollars per year that will be lost by the world's fishing fleets,[9] the effects of overfishing include substantial loss of biodiversity, incursion of invasive species, worsening water quality (decreasing the oceans' ability to absorb CO_2), and depletion of fisheries to a degree from which they will likely not recover. Most unnerving in the short-term, however, is the fact that hundreds of millions of people depend on fish for their daily sustenance, and as the human population continues to grow exponentially, this demand can only increase.

Population growth is very likely the root of many of our problems. How can our species, dependent as it is on our environment, continue to grow and flourish if the resources we all depend on do not keep pace with population growth? In 1798, Thomas Malthus thought it could not. He postulated, referring primarily to food supply, that "the power of population is indefinitely greater than the power in the Earth to produce subsistence for man."[10] The resulting crash is known as a Malthusian catastrophe.

After World War II, the green revolution changed the face of agriculture. Crop yields were substantially increased by bringing high-yield grains together with enhanced agricultural infrastructures and first-world pesticides and herbicides. As a result, countries like India and the Philippines, which were previously at the brink of severe famine, were able to become self-sufficient, feed their people, and generate revenue from grain exports as well. In this way, the impending Malthusian catastrophe was averted. Or was it simply delayed?

The green revolution was indeed a miracle of technology, but in those postwar times, little thought was given to long-term impacts on the environment or society. Industrialized agriculture is hardly what we would call sustainable. It is heavily dependent on fossil fuels for fertilizers, harvesting, and transportation; uses vast amounts of freshwater; and creates dangerous outflows of pollutants and unwanted nutrients into the environment.

Peak oil is the term used to describe the maximum point of world petroleum production or extraction. After this peak is reached, the supply can only decline, because the amount of oil and gas in the earth's crust is finite. Many scientists believe peak oil will occur in this decade, and others insist it has already passed, but no one argues that it won't come soon, except a few executives and economists from the oil business.[11] It is common knowledge that global oil reserves are generally overstated,[12] so it is likely that where exactly the peak is, will be known only in retrospect.

One might argue that, as easily recovered oil reserves disappear, oil that is harder to extract will become cost-effective. That may, in fact, be the case if the evaluation is based solely on economic factors. But what of the environmental costs? As onshore and nearshore oil availability decreases, the search for oil is pushed farther out to sea into deeper water. And even though oil industry executives and political leaders alike tell us the technology behind deepwater drilling is safe and secure, a single mistake or error in judgment can have devastating environmental consequences. Consider the most infamous consequence of peak oil to date: the April 2010 explosion and sinking of the British Petroleum drilling rig Deepwater Horizon. This accident killed eleven crew members and left a gushing oil well open for eighty-seven days to spew almost five million barrels of oil into the Gulf of Mexico.[13] In an effort to disperse the oil, British Petroleum sprayed more than seven hundred thousand gallons of chemical dispersants into the spill, before the Environmental Protection Agency insisted that less toxic alternatives to the selected dispersant be found.[14] This was the largest spill in the history of oil drilling and the worst environmental catastrophe to date in U.S. history. It will take decades before the world knows the full extent of the environmental consequences resulting from the Deepwater Horizon spill, but the preliminary estimates are no less than ominous.

Oil extracted from oil shale and tar sands is economically viable only if oil prices are high. That is because this oil is expensive to extract. It must be cooked out of the sands, and the industrial extraction process itself requires tremendous amounts of natural gas (used to melt the oil out of the sand) and water, and tends to degrade large areas of formerly undeveloped boreal forest and tundra. The lunacy of this is well-expressed by Rob Hopkins in *The Transition Handbook: From Oil Dependency to Local Resilience*, who likens extraction of oil from tar sands to squeezing thirty years of spilt beer from the sawdust of a pub floor.[15] Something only a desperate alcoholic would do.

The ramifications of oil depletion (what happens after the peak is passed) are far-reaching and potentially devastating to the way of life to which most of us have become accustomed. The cost of energy will increase, because most of our energy is produced by burning fossil fuels. And perhaps even more insidious is the likelihood that, as supplies go down, prices of all things petroleum-related will go up sharply. Oil is an ingredient for plastics, cosmetics, medications, and fertilizers. Indeed, it's difficult to imagine a world without oil. There will be widespread humanitarian costs: as oil prices rise, the price of food increases, and these increases are deeply felt in poor countries. Availability of food may decrease globally, leading to widespread famine, the potential destabilization of governments, and the increasing possibility of wars over access to natural resources.

To mitigate these effects, we will need twenty years' lead time before the point of peak oil is reached, to find alternative and renewable solutions to our petroleum dependence.[16] If the peak has already passed or will occur in this decade, that opportunity has been passed and our civilization will probably change substantially before our societies are able to refuel.[17] There is now much discussion in the United States about government and private investment in renewable energy infrastructure and technology. A positive sign to be sure, but this is only the beginning of that process, and it has probably started too late to stave off some of the predicted impacts on the current way of life.

Some think nuclear energy will be our salvation. This is predicated on several assumptions. First, that the safety issues that led to Three Mile Island and Chernobyl can be managed effectively. Second, that nuclear proliferation and the security risks associated with weapons-grade nuclear materials can be mitigated. Imagine a world where terrorists had easy access to radioactive waste that could be used in low-tech, yet quite destructive, "dirty bombs." Third, it is predicated on the assumption that uranium, on which the entire industry depends, is available. Like oil and natural gas, uranium is not limitless.

A final issue of grave concern is that of global security. In his 2009 testimony before the U.S. Senate Foreign Relations Committee, retired Vice Admiral Dennis McGinn warned of risks and vulnerabilities from a changing global climate.[18] World shortages of water and food will likely increase, eroding political stability in countries where governments are not able to keep pace with the essential needs of their people. Access to fossil fuels necessary to maintain effective military forces will require an increasing and unsustainable transfer of wealth to oil-producing nations, many of which are hostile to the United States and its allies. Border conflicts will spread, further taxing international military capacities. Changing climate will also stress the efficiency of weapons platforms and military support structures. McGinn spoke on behalf of the Center for Naval Analyses' Military Advisory Board, whose members are all distinguished and high-ranking officers from the U.S. military establishment. While his testimony was decidedly from an American national security perspective, the risks and impacts he described will doubtless affect all nations and peoples. McGinn's testimony and the Center for Naval Analyses' reports illustrate how climate change and declining energy reserves are dangerous trends, and not solely for environmental reasons.[19]

Finally, let's consider what the combined effects of the diverse challenges we've outlined might be to the environment. In a recent publication, Jeremy Jackson looked at the synergistic effects of stressors—including overfishing, acidification, warming, pollution, and invasive species—on the health of our oceans. The study looked at four major ecosystems, of which coral reefs and coastal seas and estuaries were found to be critically endangered, continental shelves endangered, and open oceans threatened.[20] Humanity's destructive lifestyle has led to a 50–90 percent reduction in many fish populations from estimated historical levels, the death of 50–75 percent of coral reefs worldwide, hypoxic "dead zones" near many river outlets, introduction of destructive invasive species, the filling of part of the North Pacific Ocean with floating plastic trash,[21] frequent toxic algal blooms, and increasing human and wildlife diseases. Keep in mind this list does not even address terrestrial ecosystems, where a whole new set of issues becomes relevant.

This is sobering stuff. The evidence of trouble on many levels is overwhelming, and much of it points to environmental and economic stressors that are happening now. This, then, is not a problem for our children's children, but a problem we all must address immediately. These are not national issues but pressing global ones in need of expedient solutions.

We do not think there is some magical environmental education solution that will cure these anthropogenic ills. Nor do we know of any quick or all-encompassing fixes that might facilitate the integration of the ideas and concepts we outline in this book. The solutions are as diverse and complicated as the problems we hope they will remedy. Climate change affects everyone at the same time, but how societies react to its effects differs greatly by culture, economic status, location, and other variables yet unforeseen. Because we do not expect change to come initially from political institutions, we think it will have to grow from the grassroots efforts of teachers, administrators, students, and parents. And it will require flexibility and open-minded evaluation on a local scale in order to identify and refine the ideas and practices that take hold and produce results in a given community.

Mitigation of impending environmental impacts will require an unprecedented effort on the part of all of earth's citizens. It will require the public to possess the intellectual tools necessary to understand and evaluate issues, and to compare sources and dig deeper into problems so as to differentiate truth from propaganda. It will require pushing the envelope of our human ingenuity and working together to create new technologies that can benefit us all. It will require that the people insist that political and business leaders move decisively to reduce greenhouse gasses and protect and conserve existing resources. In short, it will require an informed and stimulated populace. We believe the primary responsibility for making this happen falls on education, because only a decided change in human behavior will bring positive results in the short-term.

Economist Herman Daly has said, "If you jump out of an airplane you need a crude parachute more than an accurate altimeter. And if you also take an altimeter with you, don't become so bemused in tracking your descent that you forget to pull the ripcord."[22] The point of Daly's statement is that, if we wait for the empirical evidence to come in, it will probably be too late to make choices.

CHAPTER TWO

Foundations

Environmentalism is not an option like choosing one's religion or political affiliation. It is a responsibility and fundamental aspect of cohesive society, like respect for the law. It isn't something we should debate teaching. If we breathe, if we consume anything, then we are each responsible for our part in that consumption, like it or not. That society has failed to accept this responsibility is a result of placing ourselves at the center of our universe and believing we are here to dominate our surroundings. Unfortunately for where we find ourselves today, the concept that "man is the master of all he surveys" is at the root of most of what is taught in our schools. It is an idea that permeates our approach to education, and the authors believe it represents a flawed logic that has outlived its utility.

We are always ready to applaud human ingenuity as the means by which our societies have grown and flourished, and we are mostly right in that celebration. We are, after all, remarkable creatures in our ability to reason and choose, to create art and literature, and to hone our minds to perform critical scientific analysis. We have mastered agriculture, literally moved mountains, and made habitable space where before there was only sea. No other species on earth shares our incredible potential to change our surroundings to suit our needs. The industrialization of our societies is what we consider the crown jewel in the story of our development.

Who can blame the founders of our industrial society for their aspirations for its growth? More of any good thing always seems like a great idea. As the Industrial Revolution progressed, life generally got easier for large segments of our population, especially for the newly formed middle class. Motorized transport replaced horse and cart, more goods were available in more places, and for perhaps the first time in our history common folk found themselves with leisure time on their hands. In times of plenty like those at the dawn of industrialization, it would have been difficult to imagine any negative consequences. In fact, it's taken more than two hundred years for us to begin to recognize the detrimental effects of our unbridled industrial expansion.

We cannot dismiss the benefits of that innovation in the form of increased comforts and quality of life, which seem to go hand in hand with development. Advances in the fields of medicine and technology have led to increased longevity and a more active populace, at least in more affluent countries. At the outset of the industrial revolution, when world population was still well under the two-billion mark, who could have known our resources were finite, or that industrial development would have a species-threatening dark side?

Yet, even at the turn of the last century, in response to a rapidly urbanizing America and the loss of individuality through the industrial revolution, the "nature study movement" was born.[1] Its advocates were the first to include environmental education as part of school curricula, and it became mandated in a few states. Learning about nature was an essential part of a progressive education. John Dewey, the great progressive educator and one of America's most notable philosophers, believed that, by studying nature, students would develop not only an aesthetic sense but an ethical sensitivity as well. The movement's goal was to take students outside and allow them to imagine a natural world, a world without people, a world before industrialization. By doing so, students would become more grounded and respectful of nature. The nature study movement encouraged students to plant school gardens in order to grow closer to nature and to ward off what the movement perceived as the isolation caused by urbanization and industrialization.

As the nature study movement grew, adults became interested in studying and reading about nature. Authors like Henry David Thoreau and John Muir wrote books that were devoured by the public, perhaps much as nature documentaries are today.[2]

In many respects, the nature study movement was antiscientific in that it focused on developing a moral link to nature, the consequences of which would, its proponents hoped, result in nature's preservation.

The nature study movement died when many Progressive Era reforms died. It failed in the trenches of World War I, as conservation was redefined to reflect the valuation of efficiency over natural diversity. Using natural resources to support the war effort was more important than saving natural resources. Yet its failure was not complete: it inspired midcentury conservationists, who have had a much more direct impact on our current thoughts on nature conservation, biodiversity, and environmental education.

By the mid 1930s, Aldo Leopold was expressing ideas that would later be published in *A Sand County Almanac*. In this book, Leopold shared his observations of nature—to which he was deeply and poetically connected—under the threat of overuse, mismanagement, and pollution. He witnessed the disappearance of wilderness and mourned the loss of the harmony he believed must exist between man and land. He saw this harmony as based on acceptance and appreciation of an interrelationship he believed existed between living things and their environment. He gained his perspective from contemplative interaction with his surroundings, understanding nature as admirer, hunter, farmer, and protector, rather than as an impartial and disconnected observer. Aldo Leopold is considered by many to be the father of land conservation and management movements. He remains a major influence in the field, although at the time he lived, his efforts toward local conservation were not particularly lasting or widespread.

In 1962, Rachel Carson, a fisheries biologist turned nature writer published *Silent Spring*, based on her research into the ill effects and overuse of pesticides. Although the book has become one of the cornerstone publications of environmental awareness, it was strongly contested at the time of its publication. Carson was publicly attacked both personally and professionally, primarily by chemical industry representatives, in an attempt to discredit her findings and keep them from public view.[3] In the final analysis, however, Carson's work was reviewed by President John F. Kennedy's Science Advisory Committee and found to be both credible and timely. The subsequent publicity surrounding the publication of *Silent Spring*, along with the recommendations spurred by Carson's claims, eventually led to a nationwide ban on DDT and a new public awareness of the dangers of pesticide overuse. The controversy over the book marked the dawn of industry's fight against the dissemination of scientific discoveries critical of industrial practices, especially when those practices were proved to cause adverse environmental impacts. This was the beginning of the politicization of environmentalism.

Being an "environmentalist" increasingly became associated with liberalism, perhaps partly because slogans like "Ecology Now" were a familiar rallying cry of the counterculture of the 1960s, which was also characterized by its strong antiwar and antiestablishment sentiments. The potential negative economic impacts that environmental protective legislation stood to make on conservative stronghold professions like logging and industrialized agriculture and fishing may have also spurred something of a backlash, further adding to the characterization of environmentalists as liberals. This was a windfall to those who would benefit from the imposition of lesser or no regulations on industry, because it meant that the general public was less likely to take the issues seriously if they could be framed as the collective ravings of a bunch of "tree-huggers."

As ideological divisions between liberals and conservatives widened, environmentalists were increasingly marginalized, until the word *environmentalist* became synonymous with a fringe element. This effectively meant that many underlying environmental issues, being easier to discount, were marginalized along with the environmental movement.

It is already difficult in our world to understand where the truth of any given situation lies. We are pulled in many directions by governments, media, and religious leaders, to name but a few of the factors in play. Even if we are willing to invest the time to understand an issue, we often encounter views diametrically opposed to each other from seemingly legitimate sources, making it even harder to know what is true and what is not. As a result, news regarding adverse anthropogenic impacts on the environment, along with the long-term ramifications, has been largely discredited or ignored altogether by the general public until quite recently. Even now, in the face of overwhelming scientific evidence to the contrary, there are many who still believe global warming either doesn't exist or poses no threat and isn't worth worrying about. And without pressure from their constituents, politicians are unlikely to focus their attention or legislative efforts on environmental issues.

In 2002, the No Child Left Behind Act (NCLB) was signed into law. The law represented a sweeping federal attempt at educational reform through implementation of standardized achievement testing in public schools, which was designed to compel schools to reach standards set by the individual states. The intent was to raise student performance in subjects like math, English, and science, as well as to increase institutional accountability. This was to be accomplished by the annual yearly progress requirement, which mandates that test scores must continue to increase over those of preceding periods, promoting and assuring better institutional performance. In theory, schools that failed to make annual yearly progress would be placed on a "failing schools" list and eventually would either improve or close. In practice this has not been the case.

While there is much ongoing debate on whether the NCLB Act is worthwhile, its negative impact on environmental education has been substantial. Teachers, under the NCLB Act, have been constrained to "teach to the tests," which means there is increased emphasis in the classroom on making sure students prepare primarily for the subjects on which they will be tested. This has led to an effective decrease in environmental education because it is not a subject that the architects of the NCLB Act care much about. As a result, environmental literacy has suffered at the precise moment when society stands to benefit most from increased awareness of environmental issues and causes.[4]

For the coming environmental challenges to our ways of life, we need to abandon the current definition of environmentalism with all its connotations. We must realize we all breathe the same air, drink the same water, need to eat, and need shelter from the elements. We must accept that we are each individually responsible for making sure we do no irrevocable harm to the natural systems that support us.

This collective responsibility has nothing to do with liberal or conservative values. In no way does it conflict with religious or lifestyle choices. It is not a political issue and should not be treated as such. Without a habitable planet, political inclination won't matter much anyway. In fact, one could go so far as to say protecting the ecosystem, and our place in it, is the necessary first step for promoting any given political or religious beliefs to future generations.

It is critical that environmental education teach the concept of individual responsibility, just as traditional education teaches respect for law and order or as religious education teaches its respective version of morality. This must become a fundamental aspect of the environmental educational approach if we are to fix the environment we teach about. Educators will need to overcome the idea one can simply opt out if one chooses not to acknowledge that environmental problems exist.

Some may see this approach as one that incorporates activism in the educational agenda and, thus, oversteps the traditional boundaries of public education. We have been told education must provide the evaluative tools necessary for students to make informed decisions and become productive members of our society—impartial tools that students can use to find their own way in the world. But strict adherence to an impartial approach to public education design does not consider the peril that an increasing rate of environmental degradation creates. This fundamental educational principle is urgently in need of modification.

It is also a common opinion among educators and policy makers that education should not include any attempt to change or influence behavior, because doing so might constitute some form of political advocacy. But there is really no difference between the widespread practice of teaching people to follow the laws of our societies (an action or behavior generally accepted as cultural knowledge) and teaching respect and responsibility for the finite resources of earth on which our lives collectively depend. Learning about our life support system is a civic responsibility.

In California, we take pride in being at the forefront of the country in environmental awareness. The current *Science Content Standards for California Public Schools*, written in 1998,[5] does not, however, specifically mention important environmental issues like pollution, CO_2 and methane emissions, energy consumption, oil dependency, or loss of biodiversity. There is almost no mention of the linkages between anthropogenic impacts and environmental change.

The content standards are divided into several broad categories, including physical science, life science, and earth science, each of which is further divided into subcategories to accommodate additional information as students progress through the educational process. Environmental science is mentioned only in general terms and is certainly not emphasized or integrated in a meaningful way. The standards do not provide enough of the tools necessary for students to practically understand the environmental processes that will likely change their world and their lives.

This does not mean that environmental education is not taught to California students. It is, but selectively, where individual teachers or charter school boards have recognized the need, allocated the time, and provided the money. Where environmental education resources exist, they tend to exist outside the system, either as elective teacher-enrichment opportunities or curricula sources, or in the form of student outdoor education programs. These, however, often require that teachers dedicate time for which they are not compensated, and many of the programs are not readily available to all students. The point here is that environmental education is not yet a significant part of the public education system, but it should be.

The No Child Left Inside Act passed the U.S. House of Representatives in September of 2008 by a margin of almost two to one.[6] This legislation sought to integrate environmental education into the federal guidelines established by the NCLB Act, create incentives at state level for development of environmental literacy plans, and provide funding for teacher training in environmental education that would be conducted primarily outside the classroom in natural surroundings. The bill was the result of a grassroots coalition of conservation and education groups. Its passage sent a strong message to government that any educational reform must include a substantial environmental component. The 2008 version of the bill never became law, but the bill was reintroduced in 2009 in the hope that meaningful legislation will follow. As of the writing of this book, no such legislation has made it through either the House or Senate committees to which it has been referred.

In California, the Education and the Environment Initiative (EEI) was mandated by two assembly bills, passed in 2003 and 2005.[7] The initiative's backers hope the EEI will lead the nation in providing environmental curricula to primary and secondary public schools in the state, with an overall goal of creating a high level of environmental literacy in students. The curriculum is based on a set of environmental principles and concepts that reflects causes and effects, which is missing from the current state science standards and even from in-depth presentations of current environmental issues. The EEI is expected to be integrated into the state science content standards sometime in the near future, although it is doubtful this will happen before 2011 or 2012, given the slow nature of the bureaucratic process. This effectively means the first students to benefit from a full EEI-integrated curriculum will graduate from public school sometime around 2022. Better late than never, but hardly in time for effective mitigation of the compelling environmental crises we are facing today.

What the EEI aims to accomplish is unquestionably worthy of support. It is the first legislation of its kind, and was conceived of and brought to fruition through the work of many dedicated and conscientious people over years of effort. The persistent delays and setbacks they encountered were a result of a systemic flaw of modern public institutions: institutions are unable to respond expediently because they are subject to the politics of special interests.

We must now ask ourselves what environmental education ought to accomplish and in what time frame? Say we exclude changing student behavior as a goal of environmental education, because we deem it to be a form of advocacy, even though existing behavior leads us closer to adverse alterations to our environment—as consumption rates and climate studies indicate will happen. Then we should ask ourselves why we are spending money and time on environmental education at all if it's not expected to change our behavior in a way that directly impacts looming problems? It is not a reasonable use of public money to simply inform students about nature without teaching them ways they can act to protect it.

Environmental deterioration does not respect the time frame of public institutions, nor does it wait for assessment reports or pilot program evaluations. It is critically important for us to recognize that the next decades are strategically significant, especially with regard to potential tipping points (which we'll discuss in more detail in a later chapter), and that changes we effect sooner will have greater impacts than changes that come later. We must jump-start institutional processes, not only within state boundaries, but at national and international levels as well.

This can be accomplished only if we acknowledge our individual responsibility and, as noted earlier, abandon the idea that environmentalism is a political choice. To be practical, we need to ask ourselves: how likely is this to happen? Even if we are at the outset of a global environmental catharsis, are the institutions of government and enforcement even capable of moving fast enough to make a significant difference in the short-term effects of global warming? Given the bureaucratic process and the array of special interests at work, it is unlikely we will see effective legislation or policy in the near future.

Our educational institutions are often large and unwieldy, and the task of educational reform is, without question, a daunting one. But institutions are composed of individuals, and individuals can initiate grassroots efforts with great effectiveness, even from within unwieldy institutions. From an educational perspective, the best hope for positive feedback in the short-term probably lies with efforts moving from the ground up rather than from the top down.

A review of environmental education must take the overall structure of public education into account. Simply shoving some environmental curricula into existing school programs probably won't help much. Environmental education must motivate individuals to act on environmental problems, and it cannot accomplish this without an integrated approach.

Our educational process trends toward specialized, compartmentalized vocational training, and programs developed in response to the No Child Left Behind Act tend to exacerbate this by emphasizing some areas of study over others. Little thought is given to teaching logic, which one can argue is the basis for common sense. History, as well, has fallen by the wayside, as has literature, through which students can learn the morality of our societies. Civics, by which we may understand how to live and participate in a democratic process, is not well incorporated into the current overall educational curriculum. How, then, can we expect our children to grow into involved, concerned, and productive citizens capable of supporting the democratic ideals we supposedly live by if we fail to provide them with the experience to do so?

The democratic system in the United States depends on an informed citizenry. The founders of the American republic believed this and viewed an educated populace as both a critically important defense against the rise of tyranny and a fundamental necessity for self-government. Thomas Jefferson was a strong proponent of national public education.[8] He advocated providing a formal education as a basis for lifelong learning, a pursuit he believed represented humanity's purest endeavor. Success, in Jefferson's opinion, was not monetary but rested on contribution to and participation in the collective society.

But success in today's societies is generally measured in monetary terms. For example, when we talk about the status of nations, we rank them by economic progress as developed, developing, or underdeveloped nations. We would not apply the term *developed* to a society that had learned to care physically and culturally for its people if it lacked economic or industrial infrastructure. In providing students with tools for leading productive, successful lives, we may need to reevaluate our definitions of success to accommodate our changing world of diminishing resources and increasing population.

John Dewey believed schools are social institutions where students learn from experience within a community rather than through abstract lesson plans that have little bearing on the students' individual realities. Educative activity, reconstructed or transformed, reveals the value or meaning of the experience, thereby increasing the ability to direct subsequent experience.

Dewey saw teachers as members of an organic community rather than as those whose job it is to "impose certain ideas or form certain habits."[9] He envisioned the teacher as a sort of guide who provided influences appropriate to the community and then helped students to respond to these influences. Dewey believed careful and sympathetic observation of the student's emerging interests, which he saw as signs of their growing power, would reveal developmental stages reached and offer a preview of what influences to apply in later stages.

Dewey also believed political responsibility rests not only on government but also on the individuals living in a given social system, and this capacity for political responsibility would emerge through the public education experience. Current public education, especially since the passage of the NCLB Act, misses these important concepts by instead emphasizing standardized achievements and short-term assessment, an emphasis that tends to further separate the goals of public education from that of fostering good citizens.

The rate of adult illiteracy in America around the time Dewey was writing *My Pedagogic Creed* was high, with 20 percent of the population unable to read or write in any language. As the twentieth century progressed, the nation's illiteracy rate underwent a prolonged and dramatic decrease, and in 1979 it dropped to just under 1 percent of the population.[10] It is important to remember, however, that these statistics reflect a strict definition of literacy as the ability to read and write simple sentences, and literacy tended to increase as public schools became more accessible to the general population.

Functional literacy, on the other hand, attempts to quantify the ability to function in everyday society and is measured by a variety of things, including the ability to read and comprehend job postings, past-due notices, and instruction manuals and to solve simple arithmetic problems. The degree of functional literacy in society is hard to calculate, considering the broad scope the term encompasses. There is strong speculation that the percentage of functionally illiterate adults in Western society has increased in the last fifty years. If true, this would help explain a decline in civic concern and an increase in political apathy. Environmental education *must* foster functional literacy if it is to accomplish any measurable impact on environmental problems.

The barrage of information confronting us today is unparalleled in human history. We surf the Internet, watch record amounts of television, check e-mail, monitor an ever-expanding array of social networks, endlessly text-message each other, and chat on cellular phones, all the while plugged into our iPods. All this input ought to enrich us, but instead of being better informed, we are becoming more frustrated and confused by the sheer quantity of information there is to digest. This invokes Aldous Huxley's *Brave New World* and what Neil Postman summarized when he wrote, "The truth would be drowned in a sea of irrelevance."[11]

As a result of information overload, we increasingly turn to blogs or television for synopses of current events and issues. On the surface, this seems like an efficient choice for a busy populace, but the media tends to play to an identified audience, and objective journalism tends to drop by the wayside. As Matthew Kerbel writes, "If it bleeds, it leads," referring to the media's focus on stories that attract consumers.[12] As a result, the gap between liberal and conservative widens, and our ability as citizens to reason and compromise diminishes. Meanwhile, we tend to abbreviate communication and summarize knowledge. These are trends that do not foster working together to solve environmental or any other problems.

The environmental problems we face have been exacerbated by the lack of definitive action on almost everyone's part. Where several decades ago one might have argued we didn't know any better, that argument simply doesn't hold much water anymore. There has been much disinformation and foot-dragging on the part of our industrial and government leaders, who have taken advantage of our shortened attention spans to prolong profiting from old technologies and squeezing the last drops out of diminishing resources. An educated and motivated citizenry would not have allowed this to happen so easily, if at all. Public education must accept some of the responsibility for failing to keep pace with the needs of an increasingly complex society.

Notwithstanding, much has been accomplished through the efforts of environmental educators, most of them working via self-organized, independent channels. The strides made in environmental education have had a massive impact on public awareness in a relatively short time frame and are an excellent example of grassroots success in the face of numerous obstacles, including sluggish institutions and political attacks. Without environmental education, we likely would not now have widespread recycling, environmental impact assessments, cleaner air and water in many communities, local decreases in pollution and urban runoff, and increased industrial accountability, to give just a few examples. But this is not enough. The successes of twenty years ago are not the successes needed today. As environmental education meets a social climate that is perhaps more open to its message, it must take healthy doses of self-evaluation and develop flexibility, as well as return to the grassroots mentality present at its birth and rebirth.

CHAPTER THREE

What Went Wrong

The *Oxford American Dictionary* defines denial as the refusal to accept that something unpleasant or distressing is true. In a generic sense, we of the industrialized nations of Earth are a populace in denial about impending environmental impacts to our collective well-being. We have blatantly ignored the bad news for decades, all the while refusing to acknowledge the unsustainable nature and long-term ramifications of our runaway, fossil-fuel-powered consumption. If only 30 percent of the scientific predictions about global warming and resource depletion come to pass, humanity will soon face profound changes in our surroundings, our security, and our standards of living. If the predictions are 80 percent right, humanity will face the new reality of an uncertain future characterized by an unprecedented population crash.

Denial and inaction on such a grand scale is not the fault of any one element. It is perhaps a side effect of how our societies regard themselves, a complex combination of factors that include our individual motivations, how our public policy is shaped, shortcomings in our educational institutions, and the profound effects of media. To say that environmental education, of and by itself, could have changed the situation in which we now find ourselves would be naive. To gain insight into how and where environmental education may fit in to a possible solution, we need to look not only at its design, implementation, and purpose but also outside its scope to understand some of the other potential causes of our collective denial.

In his prophetic, yet ill-received "crisis of confidence" speech to the nation in July of 1979, President Jimmy Carter pointed out that "human identity is no longer defined by what one does, but by what one owns."[1] He went on to describe what he believed was the most pervasive threat to democracy, "the erosion of our confidence in the future." Carter believed that Americans were losing their faith not only in government but also in education, news media, and other institutions of democracy. One manifestation of this, he said, was the fact that two-thirds of Americans didn't even bother to vote.

President Carter was speaking to a discontented nation saddled with inflation, high unemployment, and a major energy crisis. The crisis was the result of a panic triggered by increasing oil prices when supply was temporarily interrupted by the Iranian revolution and the fall of Shah Reza Pahlavi. This crisis followed on the heels of the 1973 oil crisis, which occurred during the Nixon administration when the Organization of Petroleum Exporting Countries imposed a politically motivated oil embargo that sparked massive increases in crude oil prices coupled with cuts in OPEC oil production and exports.

Interestingly, these energy crises stimulated legislation like the Emergency Highway Energy Conservation Act of 1974, which imposed mandatory conservation in the form of reduced national speed limits, and the Energy Policy Conservation Act of 1975, which, among other things, established fuel economy standards for automobiles. High gasoline prices stimulated public interest in subcompact and economy cars that were smaller and more fuel-efficient than their heavy, gas-guzzling predecessors. By the late 1970s, muscle cars like those of the 1950s and 1960s were all but gone from the American marketplace. Carpooling, increased public transportation, and high-occupancy vehicle lanes burgeoned as a matter of need. The development of alternative energy sources like solar power was encouraged by government through subsidies and the opening, in 1977, of the Solar Energy Research Institute. It was a time when public environmental awareness was growing, at least at the grassroots level. It was a time, perhaps the last time, in which our leaders spoke openly and regularly of conservation and individual sacrifice for the common good. But it is worth asking ourselves why our society abandoned the roots of conservation mentality. We had it, but we lost it.

When Ronald Reagan took office in 1981, he did so on a platform that promised economic growth and prosperity coupled with reductions in government-imposed regulations as the answer to America's energy problems. Conservation, he said, was not the sole answer to America's energy needs.[2] Under Reagan, the budget for solar energy development was slashed and tax credits for solar installations were allowed to lapse, thereby ending any significant governmental support for alternative energy development. Reagan went so far as to remove the solar panels that Carter had installed on the White House. The politicization of environmentalism took a sharp upward turn during the Reagan years, with the appointment of James G. Watt as secretary of the interior and Anne Gorsuch as head of the Environmental Protection Agency, both of whom were known for their antienvironmentalist views and policies.

Oil prices began to decline in the 1980s as a result of a weakening of OPEC and the availability of oil from sources other than OPEC producers. U.S. energy consumption, which had decreased in the late 1970s, turned upward once again. Evidently, the message that Carter had hoped to impart in his speech had not taken hold. It seemed that Americans did not like to be told they needed to give something up, something they believed was rightfully theirs. Never again did a mainstream politician suggest the public use less of something. Even today, in what seems superficially to be a kind of "green renaissance," our leaders speak of developing sources of alternative and sustainable energy, but not of reducing demand and consumption. Perhaps the real lesson of the Carter era was the one learned by our politicians: if one wants to remain in office, it is best not to ask voters to sacrifice anything, ever.

As America forgot about the lean times of the 1970s, consumerism began to grow exponentially. There was a growing sense of entitlement that spurred an increased demand for larger, more powerful automobiles, cooler air-conditioning, hotter heat, bigger homes, and more of everything. High-powered muscle cars returned, followed by an invasion of sport utility vehicles, culminating in the popularity of oversize gas-guzzlers like the Cadillac Escalade and the consumer version of the military transport vehicle the Hummer.

American homes got bigger as average residential square footage more than doubled between 1950 and 2005. Where 34 percent of new homes built in 1970 had central air conditioning, in 2004 that number was 90 percent.[3] The term *McMansion* has found its way into our modern vocabulary, used to describe the emerging trend in supersized middle-class homes. Oddly, trends show that household sizes have steadily decreased in America,[4] so it seems we have convinced ourselves we need more living space for fewer people, instead of sensibly learning how to get more out of less.

The loss of confidence Carter warned America about has indeed happened. The Reagan era ushered in a prolonged period of prosperity, but neither confidence in government nor a unity of purpose has returned. Over the last half century, the American legislative process has undergone a metamorphosis, making law makers more likely to listen to lobbyists or special interest groups than the will of the people, further exacerbating our frustration and alienation. In allowing this to occur, Americans have abdicated their rights and responsibilities as citizens of an important experiment in free democracy. Today, the importance of participating in the process of government is not taught in a meaningful way in American schools.

As we retain less and less sense of community, we tend to focus more and more on our individual well-being. Procuring the outward manifestations of success has become more important to us than developing our place as integral members of society. The accumulation of wealth, and the trappings that go along with it, have taken precedence in our lives, and we do not feel complete without money and things. We no longer strive toward moderation, nor are we developing skills for determining how much is enough to live a good life. Our surroundings, our role models, our media, all reinforce in us the ever-present message that more is always better, that wealth and the power it commands are paramount. We live in a society that has trouble accepting itself, where any sense of belonging to a common effort is muddled or lost entirely in our collective rush toward affluence.

Perhaps this is a good time to reflect on the recent wave of financial Ponzi schemes,[5] investment swindles that pay unusually high returns to investors, and whose payouts either come from the investor's original money or are funded with money from new investors. Ponzi schemes depend on continual growth to draw investors in, but they are doomed to eventual collapse. Collapsing financial Ponzi schemes offer a preview of what happens when the ecological Ponzi scheme, on which much of the industrialized world's consumer culture is based, collapses. An ecological Ponzi scheme is based on fossil-fueled economic growth that has increased the earth's population far beyond sustainable levels, made it commonplace to buy products from across oceans, and created needs for depletable raw materials. The ecological Ponzi scheme works as long as there is a new "developing" nation to exploit for cheap labor and undervalued raw materials. As long as globalized corporations can move from country to country, extracting materials and availing themselves of cheap labor pools, developed nations can continue to have their inexpensive products. The costs are deferred to future generations, who will have to deal with the consequences of pollution, atmospheric CO_2, and the collapse of local economies.

In a society like ours, which places such high value on the accumulation of wealth, any impediments to business or the free marketplace are often perceived as obstructive and are usually met with hostility or disbelief. Environmental protection, conservation, even energy frugality are seen as constraints to economic growth, especially when the ill effects of environmental degradation are not immediately detectable to the public at large. This situation is complicated by the fact that many of the scientific concepts explaining today's environmental problems are not easy to understand. Scientific and academic institutions have done little to ameliorate this problem—an excellent argument for including proficiency in communication skills in any study of science.

This chapter is not intended solely as a discussion of the United States' social and political climate, although the preceding examples are decidedly North American. These kinds of societal changes are found throughout the world, perhaps tied to the omnipresent nature of modern media. Open space on earth is shrinking; rural areas are becoming fewer and less populated as we globally gravitate toward urban centers.[6] Where the United States was once the dominant capitalist industrial economy, India and China are acquiring a healthy share of the global market. So called developing nations now suffer the same environmental growing pains that America suffered, whether they choose to acknowledge and address it or not. In most countries, including in America, economic expansion still takes precedence over environmental protection.

The human state of denial exists globally. It is as though we have set aside any common sense in favor of short-term gain, and in doing so, we no longer consider or acknowledge our connection to the earth that sustains us. We think and teach that we are the masters of our own destinies, but this kind of thinking has serious flaws, which become increasingly obvious as we collectively move closer to destroying ourselves. This is one place where education can help us make some space in our thinking for the communal nature of the resources we depend on. Things like air, oceans, and freshwater belong to all life, not to a given nation, people, or species.

It is easier, perhaps even desirable, to look away when confronted by the magnitude and complexity of our current environmental dilemma. Believing that we, as individuals, can somehow bring about change, is probably somewhat simplistic. Local recycling is a nice idea, if everybody were to do it, but that's not happening. Environmental education must go beyond recycling programs and teach us how to achieve measurable and increasing impact by reducing our human footprint *substantially* in a lifelong endeavor. It must also show us that individual voices become louder in concert, and help us to appreciate that the problems we face are common to all of us, not subject to religious or political beliefs. Environmental education must clearly illustrate that there is only one earth, and we're all on it together.

If we look to history for examples, we find repeated instances where a motivated group triggered events that changed the course of history, frequently in the face of impossible odds. Environmental education has failed to teach us these lessons on a grand scale. Even though environmental advocates can talk the talk, the scope of real and measurable change is simply not broad enough. Awareness programs and schools do not currently teach flexibility or the critical importance of self-evaluation in the process of creating positive change. If one path seems like the sure way to proceed but fails to produce measurable impact on the problems it seeks to address, it must be modified or abandoned entirely in favor of something new. Diverse strategies must be applied simultaneously, and we can learn from both the successes and the failures of alternative approaches. Such a process of adaptive management must continue until concrete results are obtained. It is not enough to initiate legislation that bogs down or transmogrifies in the lawmaking process. Our leaders' habit of engaging in endless discussion and speculation, effectively pushing any real change far into the future, need not be tolerated. But how would we know this if we are not taught it? Educational institutions have not effectively taught us to exercise our collective buying power to stimulate immediate reductions in greenhouse gases, pollution, and overuse of resources by withholding our money from conglomerates who care little for our collective welfare and everything for their short-term profits. Withhold the cash and change will come quickly. Industry's bottom line is, after all, to get the money, and money is the ultimate regulator.

In the last fifty years, our educational institutions have changed, becoming, as noted in chapter 2, more focused on test scores than on the quality of overall education, something not easy to quantify. However one defines education, we do a great disservice to future generations if we do not find a way to impart the skills necessary for living fruitful lives irrespective of career choice. Our schools attempt to teach job skills for economic success, but in the process they fail to teach aesthetics, reason, the importance of a sense of community, civics, morality, evaluation, and compromise—the fundamental building blocks on which free and sustainable societies will be constructed.

While increasing the quantity (and quality) of environmental curricula in our schools is necessary and important, such curricula cannot be effective unless they are relevant to the lives of those they are meant to affect. If they are not, this may even prevent the desired results. There is some speculation that overemphasizing environmental problems, especially for children in the early stages of development, may create a kind of disassociation.[7]

Creating environmentally aware students in a society that does not recognize the gravity of the environmental problems it faces is not likely to have much of an impact on those problems. There exists a fundamental disconnect between what we are taught in school and how we behave in our everyday lives, at least where environmental education is concerned. This is something little-studied and very difficult to measure, but overcoming this disconnect is vital. Doing so will require all the creativity, sensitivity, and flexibility we can muster. It will require the combined effort of people from all walks of society.

We, the authors, both live and work in California, where the regular curricula of some public school districts teach environmental science and awareness, even though California's science content standards don't include these topics. Some schools even offer outdoor programs. Some private schools we've worked with have comprehensive environmental outdoor education programs for students at all age levels. In working with students from our area, environmentally educated and aware as they often are, we have not found them particularly committed to changing their consumption habits or willing to sacrifice creature comforts for the benefit of the environment. This is not to say they do not know the material; they do, but it does not seem to foster significant action. Frequently, our impression has been that the more opportunities presented to students for what we think are "meaningful outdoor educational experiences," the less interested they seem to be in participating. This has led us to the conclusion that what might seem meaningful to educators is not necessarily meaningful to students, because it fails to make a relevant connection to their personal experiences. This may seem obvious, especially given that students are not usually the ones choosing what they will be taught, but it takes on more significance when we consider the fact that we hope environmental education will change behavior and thereby offset environmental degradation.

Relevance may be the toughest hurdle environmental education faces in changing behavior. It is overly simplistic to think that, because we teach ecology, or citizenry, or any of the topics discussed in this book, students will realize their connection to their environment. Effecting changes in behavior that have positive, significant impact on the environment will take much more than just curricula. Somehow, we must stimulate some relationship to nature that makes sense, given our lifestyle and career choices. This applies not only to students but to all of us. We need to care about the things we are asking ourselves to preserve.

Unsupervised outdoor play is rapidly becoming a thing of the past, and children today are at risk of what author Richard Louv calls the "nature-deficit disorder." In his book *Last Child in the Woods*, Louv eloquently illustrates how, as our urban societies progress and expand, our children are losing touch with where it is we all come from. While Louv's book deals mostly with childhood encounters with nature (unquestionably when our concepts of the world are formed), the loss of context he talks about is a problem we all face, at any age.

The majority of humanity now dwells in cities, where the closest we get to the sources of our food is our trip to the local supermarket. What open spaces remained within the confines of our cities have been systematically bulldozed into housing developments and industrial parks. Urban parks and greenbelts without economic potential are infrequent in urban planning. Even the stars of the night sky are hardly visible, obliterated by the glow emanating from millions of urban electric lightbulbs.

We work to survive, and in our spare time we play video games, watch television, work out at the local indoor gym, or surf the Internet. We spend our time in cyberspace frolicking with e-mail, text messaging, or logging into electronic social networks, where communication is abbreviated and quick. Even when we do get outside for some recreation, many of us plug into iPods to listen to our favorite tunes, thereby excluding the sounds of the world around us and insulating ourselves from face-to-face encounters with other humans. Unfortunately for the future of environmental conservation, these are the things our societies seem to care about.

No parent wants his or her child to grow up afraid. But fear has crept into much of what we do, undermining how we view the world. For parents, the world outside their influence may seem a hostile and foreboding place for children. Media bombards us with stories of kidnappings, sexual abuse, school violence, and drug addiction, leading us to mistrust anyone we don't know or who might appear different from us. We hear of wild animal attacks, threats from disease, and the presence of sleeping terrorist cells, all of which lead us to mistrust the space outside of what we perceive to be within our control. Overprotectiveness, motivated by simply wanting to protect the ones we love, may have a darker side, a societal undercurrent of fear and mistrust that it may inadvertently foster.

We long for safety and security, but our leaders and our media teach us to seek it through insulation, fortification, or avoidance. There are risks in the world, indeed, but learning to temper the exaggeration of fear with reality may help us become stronger, more compassionate and tolerant people. These are qualities that will permit a spirit of cooperation to develop and flourish, qualities that education can help develop.

Environmental education faces a difficult challenge: how to address what is clearly "the bad news" while simultaneously creating a capacity for action in our students, our citizens. There is no clear or easy solution to this, but we must do more than simply focus on scientific literacy. We must nurture the development of individual morality, a sense of poetry and literature, and a historical perspective, things that give context to our humanity. Without these, it is unlikely we will care enough to protect our collective future.

Much, however, has been accomplished in a relatively short time. Look at the vast array of environmental organizations; the segments of academia focused on environmental science, law, and public policy; and the spectrum of governmental agencies on the planet occupied with policy making and regulation of environmental laws. The very existence of these organizations and institutions is a credit to environmental awareness and the spread of information in our society. If we consider that it has been less than fifty years since Rachel Carson wrote *Silent Spring* which directed mainstream attention to the severity of human impacts on nature, the remarkable growth of the green movement is nothing short of extraordinary.[8] Why then don't we see measurable reductions in the progression of environmental degradation? Has the "environmental community" lost some of its ability to bring about change? Questions like these probably don't have answers, but there are several related points worthy of discussion and thought.

Like the labor movement that preceded it, the environmental movement took shape in an atmosphere of adversity originating with the industrial sector, which has a long, sometimes bloody, history of fighting regulation. Regulation, to an industrialist, is an intrusion and is often perceived as government's meddling in the affairs of the free market. It represents unknown costs not easily controlled and is something to be resisted with vehemence and determination. As opulence often shares the bedroom with power, those promoting environmental reform were confronted with an unprecedented barrage of antagonism launched by industry and served up via elected officials, legislative process, and the media. Progress was difficult and slow, and opponents were many and well financed and organized.

In the face of such overwhelming resistance, is it possible that the environmental movement lost some objectivity in designing and implementing its approach to outreach? Environmental advocacy groups may have overlooked the importance of establishing some common ground with the more conservative factions of society. In failing, early on, to focus on the widening philosophical and political gaps in our society, the movement itself may have inadvertently fueled the unfair characterizations and contributed to its own isolation from the mainstream.

Some environmental ideals, however, have germinated in typically conservative strongholds of society. The organization Ducks Unlimited originated in the hunting and outdoor sports community, a faction not traditionally allied with the green movement. Now one of the world's largest wetlands and waterfowl conservation groups, it endorses efforts to reduce global emissions.[9] Ducks Unlimited is an excellent example of how conservation awareness can grow out of individual circumstances or pursuits. Hunters need space and waterfowl for successful hunting, and the conservation of wetlands assures them future access to what they value and perceive as their heritage.

The establishment of marine protected areas, on the other hand, has met opposition by sportsmen and -women. One of the strongest and best organized sources of opposition is the sportfishing community, which does not want its access to fishing grounds to be regulated or restricted. But while it may be difficult to find a middle ground between those who want restrictions and those who don't, both sides undoubtedly have central and common concerns. Things like depletion of fish stocks and the potential for exceeding potential tipping points in the marine food chain will adversely affect the future of sportfishing.

Along similar lines, commercial fishers along the Pacific Coast of the United States have become increasingly aware of the adverse impacts to the salmon fishery (and their livelihoods) resulting from logging industry practices like clear-cutting, the effects of upstream pollution, and the diversion of freshwater from rivers and deltas for agricultural development.[10] As the effects of the human assault on nature worsen, environmental allies will come from all walks of life, all cultures, all nationalities. This will present continuous new opportunities to build responsible stewardship and strengthen the foundation of environmental protection. Substantial and diverse educational efforts to accomplish this should already be well under way, but generally they are not. Perhaps, as the impacts become more visible, the environmental education community should work harder to find and build on these potential commonalities. Localizing education to highlight and build on such commonalities might help forge alliances for environmental protection, whereas disagreement and hostility between stakeholders was previously the status quo.

Any self-respecting "What Went Wrong" chapter wouldn't be complete without at least the mention of cooperation and sharing—and its lack—in the environmental, academic, and scientific communities. This topic warrants deeper discussion, and receives it in later chapters, but some cursory discussion is necessary here.

There is a decided lack of cooperation within the ranks of the green movement, as is common to many political coalitions. Territoriality is partly a reaction to the perception of threat, and perhaps because many environmental organizations grew up in an atmosphere of adversity and obstructionism, this fostered the rise of competition, protectiveness, and distrust. Perhaps this atmosphere is a result of diverse ideologies and methods of arriving at what is probably the common goal. Perhaps it arises from the perceived competition involved in securing private and public funding or finding and keeping influential board members. Differences of opinion will always exist in any human pursuit; they are a healthy occurrence and, in many cases, enable us to grow and learn. But with so much at stake, the environmental community cannot afford to waste time or hard-won resources on interorganizational or interagency quibbling.

Industry and special interests do not waver in their resistance to environmental regulation and change. They collectively avail themselves of all weapons in the arsenal to hold power and influence, including retaining expensive and influential lobbyists and funding large political campaign contributions, to name only two of their highly effective strategies. And they are winning the fight so far, by maintaining a unity of purpose that ought to serve as a methodological role model for the environmental community. Failure to work together effectively toward a common goal gives those opposed to change a significant advantage and pushes any possibility of success further into the future.

When we ask what went wrong with the environment and the environmental education that was designed to protect it, there are no clear or easy answers. It is important, however, to understand how previous efforts may have fallen short, if we hope to set things right. The environmental problems we face are numerous, integrated, and sometimes subtle and hard to conceptualize as a whole. Conditions favorable to promoting environmental awareness have deteriorated on educational, political, and social levels.

Our world is an increasingly complicated place, and it is difficult for individuals to set aside the time and effort necessary for informed participation in government process. Even if the populace were highly motivated toward political involvement, the legislative process has become so complicated and convoluted that it is not readily comprehensible or accessible to most citizens with normal time constraints.

Television and the Internet have opened the doors to a flood of information, but at the same time that the media has grown omnipresent, objective journalism has suffered immensely and the quality of information has suffered with it. Even with all the world's knowledge at one's fingertips, it is difficult to know where any truth really lies. As a result, we have made it a relatively easy task for governments, global corporations, and even fanatics to present their opinions as immutable facts. This is one reason America is late in addressing the problems associated with global warming. In the face of overwhelming scientific evidence to the contrary, the George W. Bush administration told Americans the problems simply didn't exist. And America bought it.

When confronted head-on, the problems can leave one overwhelmed by a sense of helplessness that inhibits positive action. If environmental education is to be successful at all, it must overcome this obstacle and instill hope and confidence while informing people and asking them to act on what is taught.

Most of us expect the deterioration of our world to affect our children and future generations but not us. We believe that educational efforts must be focused on young people, because they might somehow solve the problems we created. But the absence of concern for nature is visible in all of us. Who we are today shapes how the future will be. Despite our aspirations or hopes, our children will grow up to be whom they wish to be, conservationists as well as industrialists. It is important that we teach them literacy, responsibility, aesthetics, and morality, and one excellent way to do that is to strive for that knowledge ourselves. We too must change if we want our youth to change. The responsibility falls on all of us, and we have not widely acknowledged it. We concurrently share a moment unprecedented in human history: we have a preview of our own destruction, or our own salvation. The future is shaped only in the present.

Our sense of community has faltered as the accumulation of individual wealth has taken the forefront in our societies. This is tied to what goals we set for our educational and social institutions. Continuing to focus education on what is effectively job training, instead of providing an education that promotes life training, is neither in our best interests nor in the best interests of our species. The trend toward specialization must not overshadow the path toward a complete and general education. We ought not to ignore poetry, literature, history, and art in favor of compartmentalized scientific study, business administration, or other professional paths.

In later chapters we propose some turning points for environmental education design and implementation. These are not starting points, as those are already a part of our environmental history, but rather ideas for nurturing a new awareness that will lead people to act and enable them to make the tools for creating change.

What message does the United States, the self-proclaimed leader of the free world, send to other countries if its people care little for the common good and everything for individual accrual of wealth? How can America expect developing countries like India or China to mitigate their growth with environmental restraint when it failed to do so in the course of acquiring its wealth and superpower status? And, most important to this text, are these not questions and concepts that ought to be discussed and debated in American classrooms?

One thing comes through clearly: either we shape our future or stand passively by while it shapes us. The first option is uncertain, the latter . . . ominous.

CHAPTER FOUR

Accountability and Institutional Mind-Set

To better understand how education, environmental or otherwise, plays an important part in addressing the potential effects of climate change, we need to know something of how social consciousness is shaped and formed. The combined effects of media and governments tend to influence how societies perceive reality. What we all believe to be possible, or impossible, often has little to do with practicality and much to do with collective perceptions and beliefs. To be effective and relevant, educational efforts should fit into the trends and rules of the societies in which they exist, and before we can make this happen we must examine the nuances of how various stressors interact to form our collective state of mind.

The documentary *An Inconvenient Truth* seemed to mark a turning point in public awareness of global warming. The 2006 film made strong, convincing arguments for action on the part of individuals and governments alike and refuted the claims of the Bush administration that global warming was a vague, scientific uncertainty. Although some public skepticism remained as to whether human activity is the culprit, there seemed little question that global warming posed a serious and imminent threat to biodiversity on Planet Earth.

Since then, discussions about the effects of climate change that have been prevalent both in public discourse and the world media seemed to shift from questioning the very existence of the threats to finding the best solutions to them and, more recently, to living with them.[1] Finding clean, efficient, and sustainable energy sources; regulating fisheries to achieve sustainable takes; controlling carbon emissions through cap and trade scenarios; and investing the development of environmentally sustainable technologies are just a few of the topics now commonplace in the news and on the agendas of governments worldwide. Most of us are now aware of our respective "carbon footprints," and the popular demand for all things green is generally increasing. Ten years into the new millennium, it seems that the era of environmental denial might finally be behind us, and that humanity is beginning to take steps to address these serious environmental problems. But are we really doing anything concrete, or is this just a new kind of empty rhetoric on the part of our leaders, pundits, and even ourselves?

In 2009 the American Clean Energy and Security Act, also known as the Waxman-Markey bill, passed the House of Representatives and moved to the Senate for further negotiation in the form of the American Clean Energy Jobs and Power Act.[2] Among other things, the bills introduced cap-and-trade scenarios for controlling industrial emissions and mandated reductions in overall outputs of greenhouse gases. The House version set forth a 17 percent reduction in greenhouse gases from 2005 levels by the year 2020, and when introduced the Senate bill upped that to a 20 percent reduction. Both versions, however, offer lower reductions than what the Intergovernmental Panel on Climate Change recommends as a minimum.[3] We must also remember that IPCC suggestions come from a consensus document and are, by nature, conservative. In light of the progression of environmental degradation outlined in chapter 1, the proposed reduction seems grossly inadequate.

As well intentioned and committed as the proponents of these bills are, legislative compromise has whittled away at what was originally proposed, undermining the strength and effectiveness of the legislation. At this writing, climate legislation is stalled in the Senate because of partisan bickering. There is a good possibility that no compromise will be reached at all. The cap-and-trade method of regulating carbon emissions has been abandoned, and many environmental groups believe that any "climate bill" coming out of these negotiations will not accomplish reductions anywhere near what is necessary to effectively and practically mitigate global warming.

The consensus among experts on climate change policy seems to be that passing any climate bill, as flawed and watered down as it may become, is better than doing nothing at all. Why? Because it would take years to draft new and potentially more effective legislation. At a policy level, it seems preferable to accept mediocrity in environmental legislation simply because it is the best that can be done at the time. The hope for real impact seems to rest in future amendments to whatever is passed, which would strengthen its scope in the future, as transpired with environmental legislation like the Clean Air Acts of 1963 and 1970.[4] Conversely, opponents of a climate bill (at least on the "green" side) believe that any future greenhouse gas reductions or renewable energy development the bill might promise will be easy to abandon down the road as public interest subsides or as the political climate changes.

Existing environmental outreach efforts are the reason that legislation like the American Clean Energy and Security Act and the American Clean Energy Jobs and Power Act have gotten as far as they have. Without public awareness and support, such laws would never have been written, let alone passed. But if the public *really* understood the gravity of the environmental degradation we are already experiencing, and the devastating potential of what may lie ahead, public pressure on politicians might be strong enough to preclude the watering down of climate bills. If it is not the job of environmental educators to cultivate this kind of understanding, whose job is it?

On a global scale, things aren't much different. The European Union was prepared to commit to a 30 percent reduction in greenhouse gases by 2020, but only if other developed countries (like the United States) agreed to follow suit.[5] At a July 2009 meeting of the G8+5 (the leaders of the world's eight largest industrialized economies, plus invited heads of state from developing nations: China, India, Brazil, South Africa, and Mexico), it was decided that global temperatures ought to be constrained to no more than a 2°C rise above preindustrial levels. To accomplish this, the G8 proposed a 50 percent cut in greenhouse gas emissions by the year 2050, but it failed to specify any baseline year on which the reductions are to be based or how those cuts are to be obtained.[6] This agreement was a preliminary step toward a global treaty that was to come out of the COP15 United Nations Climate Change Conference held in Copenhagen in late 2009 (more on this in chapter 7). But no binding treaty was signed or proposed in Copenhagen, and more summit meetings are scheduled in the future. Many obstacles to decisive international action remain, and time once again is running out.

Complicating the issue is the fact that the world has been embroiled in the worst economic crisis in many decades, and public sentiment about environmental legislation is significantly tempered by its potential economic costs. We worry about money but have a hard time understanding that the toll of inaction on environmental problems will not be solely economic. It will likely wreak catastrophic havoc on humanity.

The issue at hand is not so much the outcome of any specific meeting or bit of legislation. It is rather what might be described as the rise of the institutional mind-set in our societies, wherein bureaucracies create policy based on self-perpetuation, which does not necessarily reflect the will of the people or enhance the public well-being. By conceding or ignoring these gradual changes to the political landscape, we grant our representatives de facto license for inaction. We furnish them with the opportunity to endlessly blame legislative inefficacy on the political opposition while citing obstructionist tactics, as the process churns on but produces few measurable results or changes to the status quo.

It is interesting to note in these times of institutional mind-set, when bellicose deliberation often takes the place of decisiveness, American legislators manage to act expediently on issues like initiating preemptive military action against sovereign nations and enacting legislation to bail out foundering private financial institutions and insolvent automobile manufacturers. They have, however, been unable to make real progress on *effective* greenhouse gas reductions or the creation of *any* energy conservation programs to effectively address short-term energy woes. When large and powerful business interests (the "special interests" mentioned earlier) have something to gain from legislation, it moves quickly through the process. When laws for the common good might obstruct or inhibit those same special interests, progress tends to bog down. Yet there is little individual accountability, and legislators successfully claim that the overall process is the reason for delays or inaction. This could only occur in an ambience of public malaise, the responsibility for which rests partly with public educational systems.

People seem to have accepted the idea the political process is slow, flawed, and subject to the whims of special interest groups. And people seem content that they do not have much real say in things, tending to direct attention elsewhere rather than putting in the work necessary to fix political processes in need of repair. In democratic systems, we still have power over our elected representatives, but that is of little import if we continue allowing ourselves to be convinced otherwise. If "democratic" governments now act first in the interests of large corporations, rather than in the interests of their people, it is only because the people do not compel them to do otherwise.

Government institutions no longer make a significant effort to disseminate information to the public in a way most people can understand. Take, for example, the Waxman-Markey bill. When it was introduced in mid-May 2009, the bill numbered 932 pages in length. By the time it passed through the various committees and the House, and was submitted to the Senate on July 6, 2009, it was 1,428 pages long. It grew 496 pages in thirty-five days, or 14.17 pages per legislative day. It is not difficult to understand why the public is not well informed on this issue. For comparison, Thomas Jefferson drafted *A Bill For Establishing Religious Freedom* in 1777 that passed the Virginia legislature, becoming state law in 1786. It was an important bill, considered to be the precursor to the religious clauses of the First Amendment of the Constitution of the United States. It guarantees freedom of religious practice and separation of church and state. In modern format (letter size paper, twelve-point type, double-spaced), the bill is three pages long.

The nature of modern politics, with its special-interest-sponsored lobbyists and spin doctors, makes it difficult to objectively grasp what any piece of legislation really means. And if that's not bad enough, consider the common congressional practice of tacking items onto legislation having little or nothing to do with the bills themselves as concessions to gain legislative support. Any potential for clarity and transparency goes out the window. The public has gradually accepted the resulting legislative complexity, and individuals interested in the goings-on of government now look to political leaders or pundits for summary clarification of issues. Given the rampant partisanship in government today and the concurrent decline of objective journalism, truth gets lost somewhere in the mix.

Recent polls show that an increasing number of people now obtain their news from the Internet rather than newspapers.[7] Television is still the primary source of news for most people, but that is rapidly changing in favor of the Internet, especially among younger people. Although much of the news found on the Web and television comes from traditional journalistic sources like objective investigative reporting, the nature of the news is changing as well. Much of what we now see on television news reports or find in the blogosphere is reaction, speculation, and opinion on what the implications or significance of any given occurrence might be. These reports and blogs are essentially a one-way forum for closed discussion, rather than a means of objectively informing the populace of events, facts, and developments important to understanding and perhaps improving the world. In the current format of mainstream news reporting, it is difficult to distinguish between what is news and what is spin or speculation. The situation is exacerbated by the tendency of our society to regard media as authoritative and subsequently ascribe a high truth-value to what we see on the Internet or television.

In most modern societies, media has historically played an important part in keeping governments and industry honest by means of the independent reporting of news. Traditionally, media has followed a code of ethics that emphasizes, among other things, stringent verification of information, presentation of all sides of a story, objectivity in reporting, and never confusing commentary or opinion with the reporting of news.[8] The U.S. Federal Communications Commission used to enforce a "fair-and-balanced" requirement that public airwaves must present both sides of an issue. Such a policy sought to ensure that the public was exposed to multiple perspectives. An informed society is more likely to respect novel positions or ideas, compared to one in which people are exposed to only one side of any issue. However, in the last several decades, there have been significant changes in media policies, stated or otherwise, producing a more convoluted style in news reporting that often includes unhealthy doses of opinion without identifying it as such. Talking heads have become yelling heads. Reportage often includes aggressive slap downs of those with opposing views. While this may increase entertainment value, it fails to nurture a culture that respects others' opinions. And mutual respect is going to be necessary in working our way out of the environmental crises we've created.

A disturbing development is the marked change in the structure of ownership of modern media. In 1983, the majority of media outlets in the United States were owned and controlled by fifty different corporations. By 2004, that number had shrunk to only five companies.[9] The gradual increase in media ownership by huge multinational conglomerates undermines the very nature of independent journalism. In fact, several of these conglomerates have been accused of presenting the news with a political bias, a practice that goes against the grain of objectivity, not to mention the journalistic code of ethics. This trend is significant to any discussion of environmental education, because public education is driven by government policies, and an independent media is the primary means by which governments can be held accountable for action or inaction. If this check system ceases to keep governments honest, the tendency for mass-media-perpetuated disinformation will probably worsen, further slowing real progress toward public environmental awareness or legislative action.

Another problem common to the rise of institutional mind-set is what we might call "bureaucratic assimilation," where popular challengers to the status quo, no matter how formidable, are simply absorbed into the process and rendered harmless to institutional momentum. Many grassroots efforts for reform or change, when faced with both internal and external pressure, tend to temper their idealism with practicality as they find it increasingly necessary to conform to the parameters and rules of the system they are seeking to change. As they grow larger and more influential, they require more money and influence to sustain their efforts. The increased need for cash leads to a larger administrative staff, which in turn fuels the need for even more money. As a grassroots organization grows in size, it tends to become multitiered and subsequently less agile. It focuses on achieving its original goals, which are often compromised or lost entirely in the name of more institutionally practical expectations. In other words, as grassroots organizations grow more powerful, the initial clarity of their idealism is increasingly muddled by extenuating circumstance.

This institutional mentality also affects school districts, nongovernmental organizations, and industrial sectors, leading to a general lack of direct accountability throughout. If things don't work, or change doesn't occur, any potentially responsible individual or group need only point to the "system" as the cause, conveniently sidestepping personal responsibility. It is a state of mind that we willingly tolerate in ourselves and which enables us, with a clear conscience, to throw up our hands in despair, secure in our conviction that we have individually done all that was possible to achieve whatever the goal. We are losing the ability to self-assess, to take open and honest responsibility for our failures and try again from a different approach until measurable progress is made.

Progress, and how we measure it, is also affected by an institutional outlook. One can evaluate progress from both sides of any problem. Take greenhouse gas reduction, for example: if we take a classic institutional view and look forward from the start of the process of reducing emissions, then all steps toward that end (like completion of feasibility studies and environmental assessments, passing of interim legislation, consensus building, negotiation, etc.) are viewed as concrete progress, no matter how insignificant or superfluous they may be. Progress, perceived in this way, tends to justify the efforts, thereby reinforcing existing methodology. If, however, we evaluate our efforts by looking backward from the goal (measurable decreases in greenhouse gases), we get an entirely different picture. We see that despite all the best efforts of the parties involved, we have achieved no measurable reductions in actual overall emissions,[10] which is the sole point of the effort in the first place. Looking pragmatically backward from the desired result to determine whether the means are really working is more likely to yield strategies that will work, in time to make the significant difference we need. If we trust our institutions to act quickly and with common sense, we are clearly guilty of self-deception on a grand scale. A commonsense approach must be applied to all aspects of the environmental problems we face, and this must be done quickly.

Powerful environmental advocacy groups are as guilty of having an institutional mind-set as anyone. Considering the materials they disseminate, how they approach media, and who they target for outreach, they are frequently preaching to the choir. This likely evolved out of a survival instinct and the continuous need for fund-raising. It is an expensive proposition to fight the good fight, and reinforcing the validity and effectiveness of campaigns helps to keep the donor base giving. But if the idea is to mitigate environmental impacts in the coming decade or two, far more effort must go into finding some common ground with those who do not support any given organization's efforts, in order to build understanding and broaden popular support for action and effective legislation.

To further grasp the effects of the institutional mentality on education and environmental protection, we must discuss how the funding process colors organizational behavior and program development. Systemic limitations on how funding is distributed is another means by which educators and nongovernmental organizations are drawn away from their initial focus. The imperative to "follow the money" often determines developmental priorities. If there is no potential for securing funding for a given project, ideas are generally abandoned in favor of what will bring in the cash. Conversely, grantees often modify their field of expertise or tailor their organizational focus to fit the requirements of grantors' requests for proposals, which are often based on the goals of the granting agency rather than the capacities of the recipient. Consequently, money is often selectively available for things like curricula development without regard for its implementation or *effective* evaluation, or the implementation of recycling programs that fail to include subsidies or incentives for reducing the cost of recycled goods to consumers. While the hearts and minds of funding entities are probably in the right place, their follow-through is often lacking.

There is often little beyond financial accountability built into the process of funding environmental programs. In program evaluation, much is focused on assessing the development of pro-environmental attitudes, rather than on assessing any subsequent behavioral change. Grantors may not really want to know if a program has been less than successful. This is because the decision to fund is usually made by a committee or an executive under the supervisory umbrella of a board of directors. The executive or committee does not want to go back to the directors (often their employers) with bad news about how a program they endorsed failed to meet its goals. This is especially true for long-term funding commitments. Programs often continue not because of measurable successes but because they have momentum or precedent.

A practical side effect is that excessive administrative demands often obscure the purpose for which grant monies are given. Significant resources are squandered on programs that have little practical importance or impact. To have an effect on the problems that environmental education is designed to address, the development and funding process must change. It must build on a combination of measurable successes and unvarnished evaluations, rather than on the subjective analyses of parties, on either side of the process, who stand to gain directly from the allocation of funds and resources.

Grantees are ordinarily required to prepare periodic and final project-status reports that include, among other things, an evaluation of project performance. There is little incentive for grantees to report anything other than how successful the project was, if they hope to see more grant funds in the future. In fact, in the approval process it is not at all unusual for a grantor to consider previous sources of funding as an indication of the credibility of the grantee, and this tends to place an even higher premium on favorable reporting. The very idea that the performance is to be evaluated by the performer is somewhat questionable. In education, emphasis is sometimes put on having external reviewers evaluate programs. Yet those same reviewers are hired and paid by grantees. If their evaluation is favorable and a grant is extended, they are likely to be hired by the grantees again in the future. Even in the presence of the best intentions, objective evaluation is potentially compromised.

Then there is the disposition of results to consider: how the products of grant funding are put to use. Research grants often facilitate the production of elaborate reports on whatever it is the grantee is paid to study. These reports frequently fall into the abyss known as gray literature, which encompasses original materials not easily found through conventional channels. In other words, these reports are never published in a place the public can easily access. They simply disappear, being of little use to anyone. This eventuality could be circumvented in part if grantees were required, or at least encouraged, to disseminate results through public channels. This could be accomplished in a two-step process. First, grantees would be required to publish their results in peer-reviewed journals wherever possible. Second, they would distribute the information through popular media channels—for example, via focused press releases. This practice would help a grantor collect broader feedback on a project's or program's effectiveness than the grantee is capable of providing, information that might be helpful to grantors looking to get the most bang for their philanthropic buck.

The authors each know of situations in which grant monies, usually public monies, were used to fund programs that produced no measurable result or useable end product. In the field of education, for example, there is, as noted earlier, a lot of money available for curricula development. On the surface, this seems a good, creative, and forward-thinking use of public funds, but it often turns out to be the opposite. First, there are already a lot of curricula available on almost any topic, and new material may not be warranted. Second, there is little or no centralized coordination and collation of this material, which makes it difficult for educators to find and use it. Third, funding for curricula development does not generally provide for its distribution and implementation.[11] Grantors tend to overlook the many practical and administrative obstacles to getting good curricula into the hands of teachers and students where it belongs. Lack of implementation, however, does not stop many grantors from continuing to pay for the development and redevelopment of curricula, often by the same grantee, evidently without much scrutiny on the part of the granting agency.

Any proposal for changes so comprehensive that they seem practically unattainable probably causes further retreat into the kind of institutional mentality that inhibits taking decisive steps toward solutions. So it may seem naive and utopian to expect a major overhaul in the existing political and social fabric to occur to help slow or reverse the anthropogenic assault on our environment. But we ought not to underestimate the potential influence of grassroots action. All of us must remember that our political, industrial, and social institutions are, after all, made up of individuals. If we demand change, we can achieve it. A well-rounded approach to education, environmental or otherwise, that includes developing a historical perspective, critical thinking skills, and individual responsibility and accountability will be a grand step toward countering institutional mind-set and improving our communities and our environment.

CHAPTER FIVE

The Needs of Environmentally Active Citizens

In previous chapters, we've discussed some of the problems facing our planet, and reasons why environmental education has not brought about measurable impacts on or reversals of these destructive trends. We have made a case for developing a more responsible citizenry as a central factor in changing the collective future for the better. But what does this really mean? What are the elements of the sort of responsibility that successfully leads to broad-scale action? In this chapter, we examine those elements and identify some of the traits we believe necessary to help active citizens confront the coming challenges to our planet's environment. Traits that public education must help instill.

One of the exciting and frustrating things about education is that it's impossible to teach everyone exactly what they must know. Fundamentally, educators should teach their students how to learn and how to ask critical questions. Students need ecological, moral, and environmental awareness along with the practical skills necessary to convert that awareness into action.

Environmentally aware citizens must be able to evaluate complex information and make informed decisions about things they can't currently envision, which makes capacity-building all the more important. We trust that educated and motivated citizens will ultimately make environmentally informed decisions and then act on those decisions.

We have talked about the importance of keeping environmental education relevant, which is likely the most daunting challenge for modern educators. What is taught must have real bearing on the lives of students in order to create a deeper connection to what is learned. Students need to recognize the importance of what is taught, not only because their teachers tell them it's important, but also because they come to understand, on their own, how it directly affects them, their friends, their families, and their future. Environmental educators must continually strive to "keep it real." This probably requires exceeding the limitations of traditional teaching methods, which tend toward a more abstract approach. If environmental education is to effect behavioral change, one of the things it must accomplish is to cultivate appreciation of nature, a fundamental element of responsible citizenry. The kind of education necessary for nurturing this responsibility does not come solely from formal learning.

We were fortunate. Even as city dwellers we spent our childhood exploring the outdoors. With and without our parents, we wandered deserts, mountains, and oceans. We backpacked, skied, biked, sailed, climbed remote peaks, and encountered wildlife up close. Dan remembers being sixteen and hiking alone in the Colorado Rockies, when he popped out of the willows, surprising a coyote drinking water from a stream. Startled, both Dan and the coyote immediately looked for a place to escape, but then each paused, took a deep breath, and watched the other for a while. The coyote resumed drinking and trotted calmly away while Dan watched in amazement. A simple encounter, but one Dan will always remember. This experience helped shape his respect for animals and his desire to see them in their natural environments.

Surviving in remote mountains isn't necessarily considered a safe childhood endeavor these days, but doing it taught us self-reliance and the consequences of our actions or inactions. When your rope gets stuck while you are rappelling down a cliff in a thunderstorm, you've got to get yourself out of that mess. When a dense fog or whiteout descends, you have to know where you are and how to find your way home. When you run out of food or water or shelter, you have to cope somehow. Adapting to nature's capriciousness helped us become flexible, resourceful, and competent in the outdoors. Nature provides repeated object lessons in self-sufficiency, which is an important facet of an active citizenry.

As we became increasingly comfortable in the wilderness, it was easier to see and appreciate the miraculous details of wherever we were. Any trepidation gave way to fascination and a curiosity that drives one to continued exploration and experience. Encounters with wildlife were a frequent occurrence as we learned where and how animals live. Each of us, in our own way, came to feel a part of the grand natural system, related somehow to what we saw and discovered and responsible for our part in that system. Respect for nature, yet another important element of a conscious society, is born of spending time outside with an appreciation of the value of that experience.

We strongly believe that spending time in wild places, as we did growing up, provided the foundation for our environmental concern; but not everyone has the same aspirations as we did, and public education must take that into consideration. It is also naive to expect that all students will become defenders of the environment if exposed to experiences in nature. Even so, there are numerous educational benefits to be gained from moving pedagogy outside, and a greater and more practical understanding of the environment, and our place in it, is certainly at the top of the list. It should be attempted in whatever form possible, selectively if necessary, as a key step toward nurturing respect for nature in our societies.

It would be impractical and unfair to assign the entire task of exposing students to nature solely to educators, who, for the most part, lack adequate resources to teach existing curricula, let alone spend time outside with their classes. And it would be shortsighted to say that the appreciation and awareness we advocate, as a basic element of citizenry, should be cultivated solely in students and young people. All humanity faces climate change, pollution, and loss of biodiversity together, and the solutions must germinate not only in educational institutions but in homes and communities as well. Environmental educators and policy makers should understand this important tenet and adapt the educational process to stimulate and reinforce changes occurring both within and outside the classroom.

To foster environmentally active citizens, schools can encourage appreciation of nature through a variety of outdoor experiences. Importantly, these encounters need not be isolated from the rest of the curricula. With some creativity and imagination, lessons from almost all fields of study can be taught outdoors, emphasizing practical examples as they occur in nature over the memorization of abstract concepts in the classroom. Each region and habitat has a unique set of threats, and a study of practical causes and effects from a legal, political, or economic viewpoint may help frame those threats in a broader perspective.

So far, we have written about taking students to nature, but what of bringing nature to students? Academic institutions, as David Orr points out, tend to have "the architectural elegance and performance standards common to shopping malls, motels, and drive-through funeral parlors."[1] Orr goes on to say that the design of educational institutions has grown up on the idea that surroundings don't matter and little is learned from the actual buildings in which students are taught. He suggests that the physical academic environment can itself be a teacher. Incorporating energy and waste efficiency, local materials, solar heating, and importantly, student and faculty participation in the design process can help move campuses toward holistic learning environments.

The practical process of providing exposure to nature in schools is by no means easy, but consider what might be accomplished if students, faculty, the facilities management staff, and administrators set to redesigning and rebuilding existing facilities. As an interim grassroots step, what if students were challenged to "green up" their campuses and find innovative ways to pay for those enhancements without the influx of additional monies? At best, the academic environment might quickly change, stimulating the collective creativity of students and faculty to transform schools into places students want to frequent and are proud of, and which are environmentally improved.

Doing so may also provide ideas for future institutional redesign. At worst, the effort would lead to new and more practical ways of teaching and learning about the relationship of humans to their surroundings. Either way, the process would promote involvement in community effort and good citizenry.

The concept of community has changed dramatically in recent years and continues to evolve. Proliferation of the Internet, social networking, e-mail, and text-messaging has helped to reshape the idea of community, such that Internet communities and forums are now touted as public spaces (albeit in cyberspace) accessible for the open exchange and discussion of ideas. *Community* is beginning to mean places (or sites) that like-minded people go to or frequent. This technology-era interpretation of community misses an important aspect of a more traditional definition: where people of different views and backgrounds live together out of necessity, learning to resolve their differences to maintain harmony for mutual benefit. Mutual benefit, for the purposes at hand, means the collective reduction of greenhouse gasses, protection of wilderness and biodiversity, conservation of energy and resources, and planning for an uncertain future together as a community. This requires active citizens to expand their concept of community to include people who do not share their views, cultures, or traditions, and to make reasonable efforts toward tolerance and understanding of those differences. In dealing with the environmental challenges ahead, the community is a global one, like it or not. Impending threats cannot and will not be mitigated by any single nation alone. Environmentally active citizens must understand this.

How people exchange ideas is changing rapidly in the world. Internet forums and social networks are essentially bulletin boards where one can post one's ideas, receive viewer comments, and if inclined, respond at one's convenience. Twitter, the latest social networking flavor-of-the-month is based on concise posts (no more than 140 characters per message) that interested parties can follow. The potential for dissemination of information is unparalleled in history, as was evident in recent American elections where candidates successfully used the Internet to rally support, raise funds, and spread their messages. Active citizens, to help advance a sense of global community, need to be fluent in the use, etiquette, and function of these and future networks.

The lifeblood of community is communication. It is the social glue that holds people together. If communication falters, differences become more difficult to resolve because common ground is harder to find. News travels fast around the planet, but it is worth noting that dissemination of information is not the same as communication. There are inherent limitations to communication when people are physically isolated from one another and when the very means of discourse are both abbreviated and instantaneous. Messages are more often misunderstood when there are no accompanying facial expressions and tone of voice to rely on, or time for evaluation and response; all are important aspects of effective communication. Active citizens, in order to communicate effectively, need to listen, to ponder, to respond, to write, and to read. In other words, active citizens need to be literate, and educators must make sure the measure of such literacy transcends basic scores on scholastic achievement tests and helps cultivate the capacity for critical thinking and communicating one's thoughts to others.

True scientific literacy is one integral component of this process and can provide a conceptual tool kit applicable to a variety of questions and issues. Environmentally active citizens will be fluent in mathematics, biology, chemistry, and physics. With these basics, citizens will be well prepared to critically evaluate future problems they never were exposed to in school. A fundamental understanding of diversity and evolution, for example, might yield the tools for comprehending discoveries in the field of genetics occurring after students have left the educational system. Mathematics, as well, is a subject that provides the logic and tools to understand other subjects, especially if taught in ways that highlight practical problem solving.

Nature provides a workbook in which activities in hard science can be applied to solve problems and answer questions. What is the wave force acting on mussels on a rocky shore? How do chemicals change with exposure to ozone or ultraviolet radiation? How many earthworms are there in a garden? How many fish can be sustainably harvested? How does the rate of grass growth change under different fertilizer regimes? What happens to prey if all their predators are killed off? Having the tools to thoughtfully confront issues and questions like these is essential for active citizens able to understand the consequences of environmental degradation.

Environmental education must constantly integrate emerging ideas and research that is conceptually pertinent to a more comprehensive understanding of the causes and effects of environmental problems. In recent years, traditionally scientific tools, like network theory, have been applied to seemingly unrelated subjects, like economics or population studies, with compelling results. The ability to see and understand these interdisciplinary concepts is essential to environmental awareness in the transitional future that humans (and others) now face.

It is clear to most scientists that the present level of human consumption of resources and energy is simply not sustainable. Earth just can't keep up. So the world will change, and the change will come soon. The responsibility for how society will deal with coming changes probably rests on the shoulders of this and the next few generations of humans. This is a time of transition . . . but transition to what? Whether the future is one of political instability, fraught with wars and conflict as resources become increasingly scarce, or whether humanity moves toward a more sustainable existence, is up to all of us. Understanding the transitional process is key to finding ways toward a more resilient future.

Environmentally active citizens will need to understand how nonlinear dynamics and phase shifts pertain to periods of transition. Ecological relationships are often nonlinear. This means that a unit change in an input does not necessarily lead to a proportional change in output. It may lead to a multiplicative change in output, or in some situations, sudden severe changes that may be difficult to predict. These rapid changes are called phase transitions. Water, as it changes from solid state to liquid state to gaseous state, provides an illustration of phase shifts, or transitions, that we commonly experience. At 0°C, water freezes solid; at 100°C, water turns to gas. Malcolm Gladwell called these specific thresholds tipping points.[2]

An example of ecological nonlinearity might be the melting of polar ice caps. As ocean and air temperatures rise, polar ice ought to melt at a predictable rate, but studies are beginning to show that this may not be the case. The measurable input unit of temperature increase does not necessarily cause a certain unit of ice melt because of factors that are difficult to measure or foresee. The process becomes nonlinear because, among other things, as highly heat-reflective sea ice melts, it is replaced by dark ocean water, which absorbs much more heat than white ice, thereby accelerating the ice melt.[3]

Educators might use the ecological management of fisheries to illustrate how tipping points come into play despite the best efforts of science. Virtually every major fishery humans have attempted to manage through the application of scientific principles has collapsed. This indicates that the modeling and management tools utilized were not adequate to predict the point at which a given fishery is unable to replenish its numbers. Extraneous influences like lack of protective legislation and, where legislation exists, political corruption, underlying uncertainty, and lack of enforcement capability contributed to management efforts that failed to predict a population's tipping point.[4]

There are broader lessons to be drawn from nonlinear dynamics. For instance, to get from state A to state C, you sometimes have to go through state B. Each of these states may be stable. Again, consider H_2O. Between $0°C$ and $100°C$, it is stable as water. Below $0°C$, it is stable as ice. Above $100°C$, it is stable as steam.

What are the implications of the nonlinear approach for society? Breaking humanity's fossil fuel addiction will require working through several stable states, because the technology or capacity to suddenly transform our society to one that runs entirely on renewable sources of energy simply does not currently exist. By taking a nonlinear approach, looking at one problem at a time, active citizens may find a clearer road map to solutions that span multiple stable states. Consider transportation. Hybrid technology, while it may not be an ultimate solution, may provide an interim stable state while efficient vehicles that run entirely on renewable sources of energy are developed. Understanding nonlinearity is essential to understanding environmental impacts like increasing greenhouse gases in the earth's atmosphere, warming ocean temperatures, and loss of biodiversity. Environmental educators need to work carefully to make this relevant to the lives of their students.

Teaching ecological linkages and an appreciation of the diversity of networks is also important in the education of environmentally active citizens. The human species is not isolated on earth, and our continued existence requires interactions with other species. Examples of these interactions are found in food webs that are graphical descriptions of the foraging relationships between predators, their prey, and the plants and phytoplankton they eat. The structure of these relationships provides an intuitive illustration of the many linkages between species and their potential vulnerability. For example, many species living in the oceans near Antarctica persist because of abundant small shrimplike marine invertebrates called krill. The entire network of foraging relationships is centered on krill. Whales eat krill. Fish eat krill. Penguins eat fish that eat krill. Seals eat fish and penguins that eat krill. If the krill population crashes, the structure of the food web suggests that all species "above" krill will crash too. In this fragile food web, krill are considered a keystone species because of their essential role in holding together the ecological community. Typically, in the United States, food webs and energy pyramids are taught in elementary school science curriculum. Stressing the importance of linkages between species is an intelligent next step in identifying the human place in a more complex ecological web of life.

Over the past decade there has been a revolution in the application of formal social network theory to study biodiversity, ecology, and economics. Social network statistics are an application of graph theory, the body of mathematics that studies relationships between objects. Networks are created using nodes, which may be individuals or species, and the ties or links that connect nodes together. These networks can exist on many levels and may become increasingly complex as they grow in size. Examples of networks include, on the small side, structures like families and small-town economies, and on the large side, global corporations and complex food webs. Researchers are developing new ways to identify "key players" in ecological and behavioral networks and, by doing so, can identify the relative importance of different species. There are also formal tools to study the embeddedness in a network where a more embedded node will require more ties to be broken to isolate it than a less embedded node. Understanding these networks provides possibilities for solving a variety of problems that might not be otherwise evident.

We believe incorporating social network theory into upper-level science curricula will offer novel teaching tools that integrate math into a variety of open-ended studies with environmental significance. For example, students might evaluate the network of distances that their food travels, identifying the links between products they care about and the movement of these goods. Once such networks are developed, students can analyze them and evaluate alternative network topologies that minimize miles traveled while still maintaining network structure. For this approach to be effective, people will need to know the true costs of the products they favor.

Most people believe in making informed and rational choices about products and services they purchase. Their choices are based on information obtained from a variety of sources, including product advertising, consumer reviews, what is learned in school, what the government says or allows, or what friends and family think. Using these or similar parameters to guide choices without considering what economists call "externalities" does not necessarily reflect the true cost to society of a chosen product or service. Environmentally active citizens, to make truly informed choices, need to understand how and when externalities occur.

Externalities are the costs or impacts to uninvolved parties, either negative or positive, resulting from an economic transaction. It is important to make the distinction that positive external benefits are often free of charge, and negative external costs are usually borne involuntarily. For instance, the price of energy from coal does not currently include the cost of poor health for those living near coal plants, nor does it include the cost to society of pumping more greenhouse gasses and pollutants into the atmosphere. It does not include the costs of polluted waterways near mines, or the loss of scenic beauty extracted via so-called mountaintop mining (where a mountain is carved away and a nearby valley is filled with mine tailings). Placing a value on these externalities is difficult, but for citizens who need to make rational decisions, it's essential to include these external costs into the price of the final product—electricity in this case.

The price of electricity has a huge effect on behavior. In some countries where the price of electricity is much higher than in the United States, awareness of unnecessary power consumption is more prevalent. Rooms are lit only when people are using them. Task lights abound. When we have lived exclusively on solar power, we are much more energy conscious. We shut down our computers when we walk away from them. We use lights only when required. If the price of electricity included the price of externalities, we suspect that people would use much less of it. This is important for two reasons. First, it reduces the need to burn more fossil fuels to generate power. Second, phasing into a system that runs on renewable sources of electricity is likely to be a slow process; we cannot suddenly replace coal with renewable sources overnight. Thus, greater conservation will allow us to more quickly meet the output produced by renewable sources as these sources are developed and phased in.

The price of oil, as well, has many external costs not incorporated in the $50-to-$150-per-barrel prices of recent years. Like coal, it does not include the cost of remediating the consequences of increased CO_2 in the atmosphere. It does not include the cost of cleaning up the Gulf of Mexico following the blowout of the Deepwater Horizon oil rig. Nor does it include the cost of maintaining a standing army and waging wars to secure oil supplies. Excessively political you say? Well, as Gretchen Daily, a U.S. National Academy of Sciences member and Stanford professor, noted, "Do you suppose we'd be attacking Iraq if its most important export product were broccoli?"[5] If you have to think about this for more than a moment, then ask yourself why no nation intervened militarily to stop the recent genocides in Cambodia, Rwanda, or Darfur? Of course, there are other benefits from maintaining a standing army, but some of the costs should be associated with ensuring a smooth-running supply of oil. And these costs are huge. In 2009, the United States' defense budget was estimated at 651 billion dollars, and some believe that number to be on the low side.[6] If the price of oil properly valued the externalities, it would be much higher than it is, with a likely result that the public would demand more fuel-efficient vehicles and better public transportation.

Our message here is that people must realize that externalities exist, and for that to happen, public education must teach about it. We believe that if the price of energy, on which the entire industrial system relies, included external costs inherent in harvesting energy and associated with the consequences of using those energy sources, then environmentally informed citizens would make better decisions with respect to the environment.

Another aspect of being informed requires an understanding of how environmental economics can shape public policy. Fisheries and other harvested resources are often managed in a way that maximizes the amount of fish, trees, or bears that can be harvested over some unit of time. The theory is based on population dynamics. If the population size is small, individuals born into a population will not have many competitors and will reproduce a lot. Their young will survive. And the population will grow. At some point, however, the amount of available resources will limit the population growth rate, and the rate of increase in the population will slow, and ultimately, the rate of population growth will decline. If one can identify the size at which the population growth rate is maximized, then it's possible to harvest all animals or plants above this population size and still permit the population to maintain itself. Harvesting too many animals reduces the population size, sometimes to extinction of the species or to a point where the species cannot rebound. Harvesting too few animals means that an opportunity to harvest more per unit of time is missed. The science makes a lot of sense, but politics often comes into the fray when determining harvesting quotas. This is why many so-called managed populations are pushed toward extinction.

Environmental economics has another important lesson worth pondering: the idea of discounting or devaluing future gains. Such "future discounting" makes it economically logical—if you're exclusively looking at maximizing profits, and making some assumptions about a reasonable return on invested income—to harvest a resource to extinction,[7] bank the money, and then look for another resource to harvest. An ominous example comes from fisheries. Economically speaking, fishing cod stocks and hunting whales to extinction, rather than trying to sustainably manage them, seems like a sound practice. But it is not.[8] Looking only at the economics of environmental issues leads to flawed decision making. Our peoples and our leaders must learn that it ain't all about the money. Our societies and our collective welfare depend on breathable air, drinkable water, enough food to eat, and stability in our environment. These are factors that a strict dollars-and-cents view of the world simply doesn't consider. Economics is a useful tool in some, but not all, circumstances. The problems humanity faces are, in substantial part, ethical and moral ones and can't simply be solved with a purely economic approach.

A historical perspective is essential to informed decision making, particularly when assessing the state of natural resources, and environmental education must take the lead in providing it. Coined by biologist Daniel Pauly in 1995, the term *shifting baselines* encapsulates the idea that perspective is everything.[9] This important historical lesson must be fully appreciated by environmentally active citizens so they will not be led to believe, erroneously, that what we have now is the basis for what we should strive to protect. This kind of thinking, which does not include the historical view of a given resource prior to significant depletion, is prevalent in the world of policy, resource management, and mitigation, and it must change. In 2000, Paul Crutzen and Eugene Stoermer noted that the current epoch in the earth's history should be called the "anthropocene" as a nod to the profound impact humans have had on the environment.[10]

On Earth Day 1971, the "crying Indian" commercial aired on television for the first time. It opened to the scene of a Native American paddling his bark canoe downriver. As he continues, the river gradually changes into a trash-filled, polluted urban waterway. He steps ashore to find a modern highway choked with traffic. As he looks on, he is pelted by litter thrown from a passing car. The Indian sheds a tear as the ad fades out to the words: "People start pollution, people can stop it." This popular ad illustrates the idea of shifting baselines. While today's existing levels of pollution may seem acceptable (it's what we all grew up with, right?), the authors of this book don't think it's a good idea to simply accept it as a given. Cars and garbage were not always here. Factories belching pollutants were not always present.

Teaching environmental history and what was here before the anthropogenic ax wreaked havoc on the earth is essential to understanding whether any starting point or baseline for assessment of a natural resource is valid. If societies do not take shifting baselines into consideration, then as time passes, resource baseline estimates will get smaller simply because they have been subject to prior harvesting in the preassessment period. Humans have been using up earth's resources at an alarming rate for more than a century, and environmentally active citizens must make their leaders understand that it is time to restore some of what has been lost.

How else might concerned citizens benefit from history? It may be true, as the proverb states, that history repeats itself, a scenario in which humanity plays a passive role in shaping its future. Or perhaps George Santayana had it right in saying: "Those who cannot remember the past are condemned to repeat it,"[11] which seems to base responsibility for the future on those who understand what has already happened. Either way, some study of what was, both scientifically and socially, helps ground actions in the present by evaluating the mistakes and successes of the past. Retrospect provides the key to unraveling the effects of the systematic depletion of natural resources under the slogan "Better living through industry."

We have stressed, somewhat specifically, that scientific literacy is critically important to an environmentally involved populace, but science is not enough. Science, alone, can't stimulate the mass change in behavior needed to reverse the destructive trends confronting the planet. Perhaps it is too much to expect that environmental education can teach how to live fairly and well, and by this, we mean exclusive of economic achievement. But learning to live well is also an important need of environmentally active citizens, no less important than any other. Without our appreciation of beauty, the dormant poetry in our surroundings goes unnoticed; nature will have little value to us other than economic, and we have already warned about where that kind of thinking leads. Students, and indeed all citizens, need the capacity to see intangible value in things: forests simply for the sake of the forest; the expanse of wilderness simply because it is alive, primal, and fiercely beautiful.

Morality and public education mentioned in the same sentence is often a source of controversy, because many people strongly believe that moral education comes exclusively from the home or from religion. Each person, family, community, or nation may have its own ideas about an appropriate moral code of conduct. Teaching these codes is probably beyond the reasonable scope of public schooling. But teaching about moral systems and cross-cultural similarities is not. Morality is a building block of civilization and belongs in the curricula of any responsible society. If we do not cultivate an understanding of ethics, for example, how can citizens be expected to understand reciprocation or compromise or responsibility? All are important attributes of free societies. Teaching moral and ethical systems may be outside the purview of environmental education, but environmental educators and policy makers must make sure morality is included in standard curricula.

We have talked a lot about what citizens and students need to get from the educational system to foster participatory citizenship, but we have not looked into the nuts and bolts of how that system can or will provide these things. Providing the educational experiences we advocate will require highly skilled, capable, and motivated teachers, who are arguably the most important link in the process of forming new ideas and changing old behaviors. Teachers who are at ease giving students a long line, and who are comfortable not knowing precisely what all the answers will be. Teachers who care deeply about education and appreciate its vital role in the development and maintenance of free societies. Teachers who can stay relevant by listening to their students, understanding how students perceive the world around them, and then incorporating what they've learned into their respective teaching methods. It will require teachers to thoroughly know the subjects they are expected to teach.

Most everyone who ever attended school can easily remember teachers who inspired them, those who took a personal interest or brought something unique and engaging to whatever subject they taught. For many of us, those teachers were the ones who helped shape the direction of our careers, our interests, even our lives. Unfortunately, the teachers who stand out in our memories are usually few, perhaps only one or two encountered over many years spent in school, but these are the kind of people our schools really need.

Where are these magnificent teachers? How is society to find and train them? Many are, in fact, already here. They are doing their jobs in schools around the world. Some may be demoralized by burdensome bureaucracies that do not allow them to teach effectively. Some may be finding it difficult to work in school systems starved for resources or crippled by neglect, or where police presence is a daily affair. Many, however, are out there doing their best, come what may, finding ways around the obstacles that the system throws in front of them.

Will offering more money bring in more of these talented people and help those already in place to rekindle and sustain their motivation? While money is certainly important, we doubt it is the primary motivator. We believe great teachers are drawn to teaching because they want to contribute to the lives of others by helping students and communities, not because they can earn lots of money. It is, after all, public service. But teacher salaries must be good, so that teachers are comfortable and able to afford homes, raise families, enjoy recreation time, and continue their own education. Their compensation must keep pace with the rising costs of living, and they need good retirement and health care benefits that provide long-term security. Most important though, they need administrative consistency and a solid support structure at work, so they can do what they were hired to do: teach well and inspire students to learn. We have seen great and creative teachers essentially worn down by principals who care more about following bureaucratic protocols than they do about helping teachers to provide great learning experiences for their students. Highly motivated teachers can shut down when idea after innovative idea is systematically shelved, and opportunity after opportunity is passed over because of a lack of administrative foresight. Quality educators need effective and flexible support structures in the form of a streamlined administration that is committed to the quality of education and the nurturing of participatory citizens. School districts must support and enhance quality educators by providing ongoing, readily available teacher enrichment grants that not only cover the costs of continuing education but also offer compensation for additional time invested.

But simply saying that teachers are important and governments ought to support them ignores the ailing state of public education as it currently stands. Public schools are rife with inflated and impotent administrations and dwindling resources. In recent years, many urban school districts lowered hiring standards to boost sagging employment rolls, bringing many unqualified teachers into the mix. These problems have perhaps been exacerbated by politicization and inconsistent government attempts at education reform.

President Obama's recent Race to the Top program, in which states compete for grants from a five-billion-dollar allocation, attempts to, among other things, link student performance to teacher evaluation, encourage innovation in public and charter schools, and beef up academic standards.[12] Many educators, however, believe that this might simply constitute a more aggressive version of the No Child Left Behind Act, and that it may exacerbate, rather than solve, existing problems in public education. Once again, we believe that, in any attempts at school reform, great care must be taken to assure that the scope of public education is broadened past that of a curriculum based primarily on economic utility.

While we believe education needs more money and resource allocations, we are not suggesting that good money be arbitrarily thrown after bad. There are, at this writing, several notable efforts for school reform, which include breaking up large school districts and the growing prevalence of magnet and charter schools. These ideas hold promise, but more innovations must be tried and evaluated. The problems in public education are complicated and practical ones, and there are no simple answers. The first steps toward any solution must include level-headed recognition of those problems, followed closely by a policy of honest self-assessment at all levels of the system. Those responsible for educating, as well as those concerned with policy making, must heed Santayana's words and not allow mediocrity to repeat itself.

In this chapter we have presented a cross-section of concepts that citizens require, and traits they must have, to become environmentally active. We believe these concepts will come, first and foremost, from educators. This chapter is intended as a starting point for further dialogue between teachers, students, parents, and other concerned parties wishing to create a better society. We suspect some will think this is outside the scope of environmental education, and many of the topics touched on in this chapter do, in fact, traditionally belong to other disciplines. But this broad spectrum of ideas and concepts should be combined in such a way that it is used to work toward an end result that includes the reversal of environmental degradation and the construction of the foundation for a sustainable future. We think responsibility for this falls squarely on the shoulders of environmental education.

CHAPTER SIX

Between Awareness and Action

It is relatively easy to create a wish list for what environmental education should provide, and the preceding chapter is our attempt to do just that. It's another thing entirely to see such a list become reality. The changes we propose are big ones, and the time in which to accomplish them is short. There are significant institutional, financial, and political obstacles to implementation that must be overcome, or ways must be found to get around them. We do not purport to know all the specific means to effect these changes but we are confident that grassroots efforts by educators, parents, and administrators will create powerful and efficacious methods to change our educational institutions and curricula.

Time and time again, we have heard the question: what can one person do to make a difference? If I recycle, will that make the earth better? If I take shorter showers or drive a hybrid, will that stop global warming? What about industrial emissions, or agricultural use of freshwater, or dwindling oil reserves? There is no simple answer, as these questions are much more complicated than they would appear. Think globally, act locally doesn't ring true for many people, because it probably isn't unless large numbers of people do it.

Real change will require a shift in global consciousness and consumption patterns beyond the scope of individual action. Those inhabiting prosperous countries, already accustomed to a high degree of creature comfort, will probably feel a greater impact on their daily lives than those living in developing nations. Thinking globally and acting locally only works if it transcends the individual to become unified community action. Only in this way, can political lines be crossed and world leaders constrained to serve the will of the people rather than the special interests of industry.

How can the ideas we've proposed as foundations for an environmentally active citizenry, be realized? In this chapter we look at some practical ideas for bringing about the changes we advocate, and we suggest possible tactics for circumventing some of the obstacles mentioned earlier. We highlight several approaches that may hold promise, some of which are already in practice on a limited scale; some are still at the idea stage.

To facilitate any rapid change, it is essential to go with what works and abandon what doesn't. We reiterate that the solutions are probably as complicated as the problems they address. Solving those problems will take the combined work, faith, and brainpower of those who make up our educational institutions, of our policy makers, and of those concerned enough about our collective future to work to make it better. Toward that end we suggest the following as additional food for thought.

Let's look first at some of the obstacles to the process of changing behavior. In 2009, a task force of the American Psychological Association published a report looking at the relationship between psychology and climate change.[1] Among other things, the report identified possible psychological barriers to individual action. Mistrust of available scientific information, problems that seem part of a natural process beyond the control of individuals, existing habits, and simple uncertainty about what to do, all tend to stand in the way of individual action.

The economic concept of future discounting that we touched on in the last chapter comes into play in its psychological sense when people tend to discount potential and uncertain environmental benefits that will occur in the distant future. This is especially true when the costs or sacrifices necessary to produce such benefits must be borne in the present. Future uncertainty, as well, may lead to justification to postpone action in the present. It may also translate into a sense of despair for what the future holds, leading to active denial as a coping mechanism in the present. This kind of thinking parallels the rationalizations people make in order to continue smoking cigarettes in the face of overwhelming evidence that it is hazardous to health. The potentially fatal ramifications of smoking may occur sometime in the future, but there is no way for an individual to know when they will occur, or if they will occur at all. This kind of future uncertainty makes quitting much easier to postpone.

How might environmental education address these psychological barriers or, better yet, break through them? Given the psychological similarity between how people regard climate change and how people look at smoking risks, educators can benefit by applying strategies and concepts used in highly successful smoking prevention and cessation campaigns to environmental education. From 1997 through 2003, when many antismoking campaigns were implemented in America, smoking among youth declined almost 40 percent, with adult levels decreasing significantly as well.[2] These are impressive statistics, and importantly, smoking reduction occurred over a relatively short time period. Virtually all the scientific research on the effectiveness of these campaigns showed that, when education and cessation programs were appropriately funded, smoking decreased. Since 2004, those trends have slowed, and cigarette smoking seems to be back on the rise. This is primarily the result of higher tobacco industry marketing expenditures, which increased over 125 percent in the same 1998–2003 period, and decreases in prevention program funding, probably brought on by a weakening of political determination. And therein lies another important lesson for environmental educators.

By looking at potential psychosocial impacts of climate change, educators and policy makers may find ideas for shaping educational approaches designed to reduce human impact on the environment. Ideas like using in the classroom some of the standardized language common to climate researchers can help dispel public uncertainty as those terms become more commonplace. This does not mean that one message will suit all demographic groups. It won't. Any environmental message must be tailored to resonate with people of different social perspectives, age groups, cultural backgrounds, and political leanings, based on their respective self-interests. People must grasp the personal benefits of taking action. Telling people to sacrifice something may not provoke changes in behavior. Showing them they can become leaders or role models in the eyes of their peers by being the first to reduce energy consumption, for instance, is far more likely to produce measurable action.[3] Educators may also be able to capitalize on positive attitudes that may emerge from collective public efforts to solve shared problems.

"When to teach what" is a question environmental educators must pay particular attention to. In the past several decades, children's literature has increasingly mentioned environmental degradation, often presented in simple or symbolic ways, in order to raise awareness of environmental issues at an early age. Posters illustrating things like the loss of biodiversity or shrinking rainforests often decorate the walls of primary school classrooms along with children's drawings of recycling centers or animals at risk. But ideas about how and when to broach the subject of environmental awareness are changing, and some educators believe this trend toward raising awareness in early childhood may actually cause children to turn away from nature in order to cope with the fear that premature awareness provokes in them.[4]

Developmental psychologists like Jean Piaget, Erik Erikson, and Lev Vygotsky had different but related ideas about how and when children learn, but a common thread in their work is the existence of distinct phases that children go through as they grow. Familiarization with the work of these and other developmental psychologists provides valuable insights for teachers and administrators committed to helping build more responsible societies. Understanding how motivations change at various developmental stages can facilitate building curricula that cultivates a relationship with the natural world in early stages of development, then gently introduces information about threats to nature at a developmental level where students are likely to react with concern rather than fear. Revealing how a student's surroundings and relationships affect development and learning is another way psychology can benefit educators. We are not recommending that educators take on the active role of psychologists, but a working awareness of what makes individuals and organizations tick is a useful tool for overcoming some of the obstacles to effective environmental education and action. We realize teachers are taught some of these theories, but schools must ensure that they consider them in the explicit context of developing ways to educate and motivate behavioral change.

In earlier chapters we suggested that contact with nature be an integral part of the educational experience. Rather than asserting that any single type of experience will be transformative, we encourage teachers, administrators, and students to engage in many experiences and find what best stimulates their interest in the environment. With relevance in mind, school districts can benefit from making regional or cultural assessments of activities, within and outside the academic experience, that offer the potential for bringing students in contact with nature. They can adapt existing teaching methods to include or build on those activities. For example (and we will start with a controversial one), consider hunting and fishing. In many communities, hunting and fishing are common outdoor activities. They are an integral part of United States history, from the nomadic lifestyles of indigenous peoples to the fabled exploits of famous frontiersmen like Daniel Boone and Davy Crockett. Some hunters have a wonderful appreciation of nature that rivals that of the best nonhunting naturalists we know. In fact, many naturalists we've met over the years learned to value nature during the time they spent hunting. Some gave up hunting for less consumptive types of nature appreciation, but some remain avid hunters and conservationists. We have already mentioned Ducks Unlimited, which has spent more on domestic wildlife conservation than any other private organization, providing essential breeding habitat for shorebirds and waterfowl and places for migratory birds to stop on their annual migrations. Regulated hunting is certainly consistent with preservation of habitat and can easily serve as a basis for teaching nature appreciation. We are not advocating that schools teach classes in hunting and fishing, but where these practices are common, educators can use the experiences of their students as the foundation for a deeper exploration of the natural world.

Of course there are many other ways to appreciate nature without killing and eating it! Bird watching has become an extremely popular pastime and can be done almost anywhere. There are, at last count, more than 46 million birders in the United States alone,[5] many of whom started bird watching in their own backyards. During migration season, it is common to see cars backed up along roads near stopover locations and people lined up with binoculars and spotting scopes enjoying the birds. Field trips to local bird-rich areas are inexpensive, even in urban areas. Taking students outside to experience these local occurrences can help to personalize the wonders of nature. "Birds" become snowy plovers, Canada geese, widgeons, and snipe. Each species has its own story. Each species has its own threats. Each species presents localized teaching opportunities. On field trips, teachers should consider encouraging students to follow the footsteps of great naturalists like Muir, Thoreau, or Leopold by creating personal journals, writing or sketching a record of their experiences, thoughts, and observations. Personal nature journals have proven an effective tool in helping students to look deeper and more critically into the natural areas they visit.

Walking outside provides everyone an opportunity to appreciate nature in ways that driving along the road cannot. We can each stop and look, smell, and listen and, by doing so, begin to see things we didn't know existed, like microclimates that surround a forest or a wetland, or the leks of mosquitoes, or of butterflies, fighting for position in a sunbeam. Just sitting quietly outside may teach us how sounds travel through different habitats. Diversity is visible everywhere; it is just a matter of taking the time and initiative to look for it. In the late 1930s, Aldo Leopold wrote sadly of a bus ride through Illinois on which the riders saw little of the land they were passing over, the richness and variety of the ecosystem went largely unnoticed, and passengers seemed to regard the land only as a "sea on which they sail to ports unknown."[6] Today the situation has only worsened, and little remains that connects us to the land that sustains us. Simply taking a closer look at what we all take for granted might help foster a different and more complete view of humanity's place in nature, and environmental education must encourage this wherever and whenever possible. But encouragement alone, while helpful and important, may not be enough to curb existing environmental trends.

A recent and disturbing study suggests that exposure to nature may not necessarily lead to the protection of nature. The study, conducted jointly by the Red Rock Institute, the University of Illinois, and the Nature Conservancy, focused on contributions to conservation nongovernmental organizations as a indicator of public willingness to support conservation action.[7] The results show that a large percentage of contributions come from a relatively elite group of donors, most of whom engage in outdoor activities like hiking and backpacking. They also indicate that people who experience nature through activities like visiting public lands or fishing are much less inclined to support conservation. These findings become even more unsettling when viewed in conjunction with another recent study indicating a possible shift away from nature-based forms of recreation in richer countries, including the United States and Japan.[8] The reasons for this decline are not yet clear, but there is hope on the horizon in the field of ecotourism.[9]

The International Ecotourism Society defines ecotourism as "responsible travel to natural areas that conserves the environment and improves the well-being of local people."[10] Since the 1980s the field of ecotourism has proven to be the fastest-growing part of worldwide tourism. Many programs include a social component where visitors to an area become involved in local conservation endeavors, scientific research, or habitat restoration efforts. It seems increasingly that people are looking for ways to spend vacation time in pristine, natural areas where they can feel that they can make some difference. Ecotourism is still in its infancy, and there is much to learn about how to run these programs in ways that preserve scientific integrity and do not adversely impact wildlife and habitats.[11] Operators are increasingly making sure their programs teach ecotourists how not to "love animals and habitat to death" and thus promote the protection of the areas they frequent.

Ecotourism, however, is not cheap. Trip costs can easily range into the thousands of dollars, making ecotourism almost impossible to integrate into any public environmental education efforts. Not to mention that any destination reached by plane dramatically increases each ecotourist's carbon footprint. Some organizations, like the Earthwatch Institute, offer fellowships to teachers and students alike, and there are numerous teacher enhancement and continuing education grants available that may cover the costs of ecotourism trips. Participation in such expeditions can provide excellent learning situations for teachers wishing to initiate social activism programs for conservation or sustainable learning. And, if these expeditions inspire teachers to develop new curricula that more effectively teach students about the wonders of nature, they may in the long run be cost effective.

Environmental education, it seems, must go further than simply taking students outside. We think that at the very least it must help students form a bond to nature based on caring for the outdoors, understanding one's own place in nature and the responsibility that goes along with it, the importance of biodiversity, and why some areas are best left alone. It also must teach and reinforce the concept of "leave no trace," so that students' encounters with the natural world do no harm. But how can this be accomplished?

In his book *Place-Based Education,* David Sobel describes how environmental education might be locally reconceived to teach how nature, development, and culture affect each other in both natural and built environments.[12] In place-based education, teaching is accomplished through a kind of blending of school, environment, and community, which takes form in local projects that might include restoration and revitalization of a park, scientific assessment of a watershed, or the creation of an urban garden. These projects, as they progress, often morph into social actions in which students learn skills that were not necessarily part of the original plan. Students may need to learn how to write grants, engineer and construct a retaining wall, or make presentations to local governmental agencies. Sobel emphasizes the importance of engaging students in solving real and current problems rather than preparing them for solving the theoretical problems of the future. The products of this process are localized curricula that incorporate and build on the issues, history, culture, and resources of the place in which they occur. Curricula specific to an area fuel personal connections to that area and treat students as active resources of their communities. Powerful stuff and well worth consideration!

Another thing Sobel recommends is "tread[ing] lightly when you carry a green stick."[13] He is referring to the resistance many communities have to any mention of environmental programs, often because environmental legislation or regulation has brought economic hardship to those communities. Sobel has found it effective to build on the cultural heritage of those communities, working toward sustainable practices, community enhancement, and development of area-relevant curricula, rather than imposing a set of abstract and foreign ideas the community is not likely to accept. This further supports our opinion that environmentalism as a label ought to be abandoned, and the environmental community ought to be the ones working hardest to see that happen. It is not a religion or a political party. It is, rather, an inherent responsibility of all humans that comes with being born. Perhaps it is in the best interest of all of us to find another label that emphasizes responsible citizenship.

At the University of California Los Angeles, Dan teaches an undergraduate field biology course (actually more of an intensive science boot camp—or, as Dan fondly notes—a science gulag) in which students are placed into groups of three and asked to develop scientifically novel questions about animal behavior. The emphasis, in this upper division course, is on developing theoretically interesting questions, but the real point is that students identify and generate their own projects in a "real world" situation. They write and rewrite their proposals, obtaining critical feedback in the process. The class then travels to a remote field station like Australia, Kenya, or the Virgin Islands, where students conduct their research under the constant guidance of their professors. Back home at UCLA, they complete their data analysis and write their papers. Eight weeks of intensive work typically leads to a high success rate, with almost two-thirds of the projects being published as papers in peer-reviewed scientific literature. Essential factors in the success of this model are active engagement and intense mentorship, which must be emphasized in the K–12 milieu as well. Such exercises and activities allow students to find novel answers to problems they select. By engaging them in real-world problem solving, in problems they themselves have identified, students may find that they care more about the project and the outcome.

At the Ocean Conservation Society, Charlie spearheaded the development of an educational outreach program that sought to address an absence of conservation studies in professional science education. Many scientists, even some environmental ones we know, often work on very specific questions that may preclude their seeing the broad causes and effects of environmental problems. As in Dan's UCLA class, the original idea was to provide real-world experience in field biology, but with the ulterior motive of pumping the program participants full of pertinent conservation knowledge and resources related directly to their experiences in the field. The program was tried at different levels, from seventh grade up to college, and was directed at students who showed significant interest in marine biology or a related field. It was offered in both public and private schools as funding allowed. As the program evolved, it was expanded to include social-action and community outreach projects that the participants, under guidance, conceived of and implemented themselves. The thought behind this was similar to Sobel's ideas, in the sense that we hoped students would learn not only the importance of environmental conservation but also the related importance of putting it into practice in their communities. In other words, we wanted program participants to walk the walk, instead of just talking the talk.

A sea turtle biologist we know, Scott Eckert, works on a program that looks for problem areas where sea turtles are harvested or nesting beaches are under developmental assault. They then go to those areas to teach the communities how they might receive greater benefit from conserving and protecting turtles then they do from harvesting them or from overdevelopment. WIDECAST, the network behind this work, now has active centers in more than forty Caribbean countries and territories (see www.widecast.org). Scott shows communities how they can develop flourishing ecotourism, which brings money and jobs into areas where few existed previously. He also teaches residents how to conduct ongoing research and helps them obtain the tools and backing they need for such an effort. WIDECAST is a proven and successful form of science-based social entrepreneuring that is spreading. We don't think it is practical for public educational institutions to send their students off to the Caribbean (although it's not the worst idea we can think of), but educators and students will profit from adapting the kind of approach that Scott uses to develop local, more accessible projects. It is an excellent example of how science, community, education, and engagement can be combined to produce multilevel benefit to diverse factions of society.

What if ideas like these were combined? What kind of learning opportunities might emerge from placing students in charge of shaping their academic destinies thorough a practical application of what they are expected to learn (see the appendix)? What if Dan's UCLA field biology class were to include a social component in which students reached out to involve the communities they visit in their projects? Or, what if they worked to implement the local conservation of resources or the revitalization of natural preserves in ways that brought direct and lasting benefit to those same communities the way WIDECAST does? What if institutions engaged in place-based education sought to provide students with experiences outside their communities by offering them opportunities to "export" the expertise gained in their own areas to similar situations occurring elsewhere? Students might even become short-term teachers as part of the educational process. The potential for individual and community enrichment is immense.

There is no shortage of good ideas for how to change things. In the past few years, many educational programs have sprung up all over the world, mostly in the form of local grassroots efforts, some of which have grown quickly to become influential in their respective communities. This emergence of new ideas is a promising trend, and support for these programs must grow globally. From what we have read and observed, it seems the most successful efforts include encouragement of imagination and open-minded experimentation, encounters with nature on some level, hands-on participation in projects related to sustainability or ecological systems, motivated teachers, and community involvement and support. These components, we believe, are all necessary elements in creating educational programs that are truly relevant to the lives of the program participants. We strongly believe the engagement and personalized meaning that these kinds of programs can bring about are essential in turning the tide on anthropogenic degradation of the planet.

Before moving ahead, let's clarify what we mean by engagement, and what responsibilities engagement might create for educators. Consider that environmental awareness may not lead to action at all. Instead it may be some combination of personal involvement and emotional investment that prompts people to act, and environmental awareness may only help frame how they will act. If this is true, and action is the goal, educational efforts will have to bring students around to where they feel a personal commitment to a given project or topic. This requires far more than teaching abstract concepts or assigning lab experiments; it requires activities that students want to be involved with. To captivate student attention and stimulate commitment, educators must support projects that are fun and exciting, that directly affect the quality of students' lives, and most important, that have a clear and measurable impact on something the students care about. This probably demands that students play a participatory role in the conceptualization or selection of any project or program. Educators must remain flexible enough to supply this opportunity to students, thereby providing a critical first step toward emotional investment.

Effective engagement requires risks and rewards. In planning or developing new projects, attempts should be made to keep projects feasible, but planners and advisors must remember that goals often change in midstream, and end results are not always what was expected. Additionally, project planners may be limited by their own frames of reference and may underestimate what can be accomplished by a group of motivated students. As a result, they must buy into the risks as well, keeping in mind that the learning process includes setbacks as well as successes. In other words, the risks students and their teachers take on with involvement in a project must be real, and the rewards must be too.

Rewards can be substantial. After the Los Angeles riots of 1992, students from Crenshaw High School, in an effort to help rebuild their community, planted a two-acre fruit and vegetable garden on an abandoned lot adjoining the school. The project grew into a student-run company named Food From the Hood.[14] As the company grew, it donated 25 percent of what the students grew to needy people in the community. The balance of fresh goods, along with salad dressings developed by students, were sold nationwide for profit, with half the proceeds going to the operation of the company and the other half allocated to scholarships for student program managers. Over the life of the project, scholarship awards exceeded $250,000.

We believe one of the primary reasons that Food From the Hood was so successful was that it was open-ended. No one at its inception had any idea it would grow as it did. Students and involved teachers alike had to learn, on the fly, how to deal with the challenges of running a fast-growing business. Goals were adjusted as the project took on a momentum of its own. Food From the Hood became a remarkable example of team effort, rewarding participants with a level of practical confidence unlikely to occur through purely academic endeavors. Students made the program successful, but, without the unwavering support, original thinking, and commitment of teachers, advisors, and administrators, the level of success would have been harder to achieve.

So when we talk about engagement, we mean an adventurous sense of emotional investment and commitment on the part of students and educators as a team, to a project for which the end results are not necessarily foreseen. Seeing an idea through from concept to reality is a powerful experience. The process promotes creativity, resourcefulness, discipline, and perseverance. It requires the integration of knowledge across disciplines, as well as leadership and communication. It is a wonderful preparation for life. We strongly believe the gray area that exists between awareness and action can only be bridged by the enthusiasm and passion this kind of engagement provokes.

In the years after the Food From the Hood program ended, school and community gardens have become increasingly popular in urban and rural communities alike. As a teaching environment, gardens provide access to the complete ecological cycle of growing food. They are an exercise in sustainability. Paired with field trips to natural areas or local farms, gardens can be a remarkable teaching tool as well as an excellent means for generating the sort of engagement we mentioned earlier in the chapter.

Growing food can personalize the message that maintaining diversity and productivity requires effort. Sadly, growing up in our increasingly urbanized world, many people never actually see where their food comes from. Kitchen gardens, school gardens, and urban gardens help solve this problem and can reconnect students to nature in a very basic way. Growing food provides practical lessons about pest management. For example, is it OK to kill invertebrate pests? What about vertebrate pests? What kinds of poisons are used? How are poisons retained in the environment? What are their consequences when they are contained in the food you eat? The more that is learned about toxic chemicals, especially those retained in body fat, the more likely society is to understand that perhaps there are no safe levels of exposure to toxic chemicals. Through practical application and analysis, students may better see the need to find new solutions to old problems.

Augmenting a school's food service with fresh food, grown in school gardens or obtained from local farmers, is another way that gardens can enrich the lives of students on many levels. Students can be directly involved in food preparation through kitchen classes that focus on healthy, tasty alternatives to junk food. They can learn about waste management issues, composting, and ways to reduce nonrecyclable by-products via active participation in management of school gardens and food services. They can visit local farms to see how food is grown on a larger scale or participate directly in researching and obtaining local foods and products for school lunch preparation. This can also help students to understand sustainable farming practices, and it can also shed light on the true meaning of organic foods.

Garden programs in schools can also be very effective in changing the way society thinks about food. Rising rates of diabetes, and dramatic increases in the number of overweight children in schools, are good arguments for rethinking nutritional practices on a broad scale.[15] Strong, healthy bodies make for strong, healthy minds, and it's time public education administrators put this idea into practice in a complete and meaningful way. An hour of physical education a day obviously isn't cutting it. The Center for Ecoliteracy has been consistently ahead of the curve on issues regarding school lunch programs and schooling for sustainability and provides a wealth of resources for anyone interested in delving deeper into these important issues (see www.ecoliteracy.org).

Like gardens, habitat restoration programs or watershed studies are teaching vehicles with the added benefit of putting students in touch with nature. For schools in rural areas, or communities near undeveloped lands or oceans, programs like these are easier and less expensive to implement than in city centers. Taking a group of students for a walk in the woods can be a great learning experience, but what if the woods are hundreds of miles away? How can nature appreciation be cultivated in bustling urban centers that continue to grow at record rates? We have read that an empty lot or city park can provide a place to experience nature, a place where teachers can focus on the micro ecology to illustrate diversity. We are not sure, however, that encounters like these build a bond with nature strong enough to seed personal action sufficient to help protect nature. In some of the urban areas where we've worked, it just isn't safe enough to take students to an empty lot or park, and we could see little reason why students might care about anything other than their own safety. Nature seemed a long way off, and we felt almost hypocritical trying to teach about protecting a natural world that these students have never seen.

For some of us, the grandness of nature helps us understand our place in the scheme of things. Some of us find it calming to be a part of something much greater, an integral part of nature. But in some empty lot downtown, as endless lines of diesel trucks roll past on the freeway, this grandness might not be so evident or life-changing. We think it's important, especially in urban centers, that students make regular field trips to natural areas from an early age, so they can experience nature's grandness firsthand, which will perhaps open a door to a different perspective.

In the past several decades, a wide variety of outdoor-education schools, centers, and agencies have emerged all over the globe. Unfortunately for the purposes of public education, most are private. In the United States, some urban school districts have experiential learning centers or residential camplike schools that classes, accompanied by their teachers, may attend on a special program basis. Costs of such programs are often minimal, as the facilities are provided by the school districts that make use of them. In Los Angeles, the Clear Creek Center is located on national forest land a few hours away from the city, and offers programs that encourage nature appreciation through hiking, wildlife encounters, stargazing, and natural science studies. The good news is that facilities like these can provide a gateway to nature for students lacking the means to attend private programs. The bad news: even when these facilities are available, actually getting students to them is difficult. Often a substitute teacher must be hired for the day to take care of students who are not allowed to go on the trip because their parents don't believe field trips are useful. The *really* bad news: there are simply not enough of such facilities to go around, and the opportunities to use them are not available to all.

Nonprofit and community organizations often provide resources and activities like cleanups, revitalization efforts, and nature walks, although these are mostly extracurricular. Many environmental organizations also provide in-service presentations and supporting curricula either free or at nominal cost to schools. Programs like these can be helpful to educators attempting to jump-start environmental education through grassroots effort in schools where none currently exist, but they should not substitute for the aggressive, coordinated, and systemic approaches we are advocating.

All people share the current opportunity to change our collective future for the better, but the longer we all wait, the less effective our efforts will be, at least in the short term—the coming century. There is a disconnect between being environmentally aware and acting definitively to protect the environment, biodiversity, and our societies. And this is precisely what has to be addressed with fresh ideas, objectivity, and cooperation, in homes, schools, and communities, in any way that works.

CHAPTER SEVEN

A Political Primer

To become environmentally active, environmentally aware citizens must understand how political decisions are made. How does environmental legislation really get passed? Why do polluting industries seem to have such a strong influence on the outcome? How can educated citizens help create environmentally sustainable legislation?

Although this chapter is framed by a decidedly American political perspective, as both authors live and work in the United States, we will attempt to take a global view as we look at these and other questions. We will offer some remarkable examples of how citizens around the world have changed seemingly entrenched policies. We also hope to shed some light on an unpleasant truth: those with money make policy. But first things first.

In a democracy, each person has a vote, while in a democratic republic or representative democracy each person votes for representatives who then vote on their behalf. The founding fathers of the United States were clear about their intentions to have a decision-making class (Congress) that represented both the states (via senators) and the people (via representatives). They wanted these senators and representatives to represent "a great body of the society," and they wanted to avoid creating hereditary nobles (as seen in other countries).[1] They were also clear about their intentions to have legislative, executive, and judicial branches offering checks and balances, which they thought would lead to reasoned decisions and legislation.

The Federalist Papers (particularly the tenth and the thirty-ninth) explain the rationale behind the U.S. Constitution and remain a testament to the careful thought and research that went into the creation of the durable and remarkable document that still guides American policy. The authors of the Federalist Papers, especially James Madison, were acutely aware of how self-interest and people's emotions tend to influence decision making. They believed a democratic republic would protect this diversity and, at the same time, prevent people's individual passions and perspectives from interfering with dispassionate evaluation and the enacting of legislation for the common good. They envisioned a system of good legislators, accountable to the people, diligently crafting legislation in the best interests of the majority of their constituents.

For such a system to work, citizens must be able to properly research issues and make deliberative decisions about which representative will best echo their wishes and beliefs. They must also be able to understand the implications of legislation passed or rejected, as this is the primary indicator of the effectiveness of their respective representatives. But as we mentioned in our discussion of the climate legislation that is working its way through

Congress at this writing, modern legislative bills are complex and tend to change quickly in committee. Any ordinary citizen has little chance of keeping up with the specific implications of any proposed law. Clarity and simplicity have all but vanished from the legislative process, and this tends to undermine the original aims of American founding fathers. If, in America, our duly elected representatives are truly accountable to their constituents, why do popular polls continue to show that a high percentage of the public believes that government does not work in their best interests?[2] Something seems awry.

In *The Assault on Reason,* Al Gore wrote that the system of accountability to voters is broken because many elected officials are reporting not to voters but to campaign donors. It now costs a fortune to be elected to the office of major or to state or federal office. In 2009, Michael Bloomberg became the mayor of New York City for a third term after spending more than $102 million dollars of his own money.[3] The total of Bloomberg's combined spending for all three of his campaigns is estimated at nearly a quarter billion dollars.

The 2008 presidential election broke all records for spending. Over 1.3 billion dollars was spent by the three leading U.S. presidential hopefuls, Barack Obama, John McCain and Hillary Rodham Clinton, during the long precampaign period through election day.[4] Where does all this money come from? Donors. Can any candidate needing so much money remain uninfluenced by his or her donors? To be honest, it's probably a challenge.

Gore noted that previous campaign finance reform created unexpected problems. By setting a limit on how much an individual could give to a candidate, but no limit on how much an individual could give to a party, the process empowered political parties to dole out funds to candidates of their choosing. A candidate who voted against the party line, Gore argued, would quickly be financially isolated and unable to get elected. Gore went on to argue that this created a powerful party machine that could be led by a president. He suggested this centralization of power was precisely what the architects of the American constitution did not want. The polite interpretation of this is, that members of the House of Representatives, who should represent the will of the people, and members of the Senate, who should represent the will of their states, were constrained to work for their political party. Gore suggested this part of the American political system was thus broken.

The case brought against former governor of Illinois Rod Blagojevich in 2009 illustrates another way in which legislators may be influenced: corruption, which the World Bank defines as the "abuse of public power for private gain."[5] Governor Blagojevich was accused of demanding money for political favors, including the one that brought him down: the "sale" of the appointment to the Senate seat left vacant by the newly elected president, Barack Obama. Whether or not Blagojevich was ultimately convicted, such corruption is visible at all levels of government and is, by no means, solely an American problem. According to Transparency International's corruption perception index, the United States is the twentieth-least corrupt country, ranking lower than Britain (rank = 12) and Hong Kong (rank = 14).[6] Countries with weak or nonexistent democracies like Indonesia (rank = 143), Iraq (rank = 178), and Somalia (rank = 179) tend to be very corrupt. A sobering aspect of the same report shows that citizens of all participating nations consistently place political parties, legislatures and parliaments, and police at the top of a list of the most corrupt institutions in their respective countries. The majority of those questioned also believe the situation will only worsen in the future.

Political corruption matters. It is prevalent throughout the world and often has profound effects on the environment. Illegal trafficking in natural resources, higher levels of pollution because of permitting or inspection systems that are nonexistent or compromised by bribery, funds diverted from environmental programs to private pockets, and unfair allocations of public resources are all examples of this.[7]

Corruption is not limited to politicians but also occurs among appointed officials with regulatory oversight. And this, from an environmental standpoint, is a huge problem.

How do regulations really get written? Congressional assistants write them. How do congressional assistants know what to write? They talk with lobbyists and often get prose directly from lobbyists. Who and what are lobbyists? Typically they are political professionals gone private who represent specific groups of people for the purpose of legally influencing legislation on behalf of their clients. In America, as well as abroad, one might easily argue that the real power brokers are political lobbyists working outside the formal legislative structure.

Who appoints lobbyists? How do they make their money? Many large, private U.S. lobbying organizations and firms are located on K Street in Washington, D.C., immediately adjacent to America's halls of power. Some of these organizations represent large sectors of the public, such as the nonprofits American Association for Retired Persons and the American Automobile Association. There are also private lobbying firms who hire people to help effect change for smaller, less popular lobbies.

Lobbyists are a sort of unelected "fourth branch" of American government who do not necessarily represent the people. Unlike independent experts who might be called to testify before Congress to provide objective information, private lobbyists are often hired to help their clients achieve an outcome. James Madison, in the tenth Federalist paper, was concerned about what he called factions that might wrest control of the democratic process.[8] He noted that there are two ways of dealing with such factions: either remove their causes or control their effects.

Lobbying firms routinely hire former government officials (both elected and unelected), because those are the people with the connections, and in some cases, the expertise, to help their clients influence the creation of legislation. While many in Congress pay lip service to controlling lobbying, some of those very same people often accept jobs as professional lobbyists as soon as they leave government. Who wouldn't? High-powered lobbying pays very well. As of January 2009, the median annual income of lobbyists in the United States was $95,525,[9] but this is not a proper indication of how much money lobbyists can actually earn. In a recent book, journalist Robert Kaiser revealed that one lobbying firm, Cassidy & Associates, took in $33 million in 2003; another, the Robert S. Strauss law firm earned over $31 million in 2007. Kaiser went on to say that the $3 billion dollars officially reported to be the amount lobbyists spent in 2007 alone, buying influence and shaping legislation, is likely a vast understatement.[10] In a national scandal that brought down several prominent members of Congress, disgraced lobbyist Jack Abramoff was paid a total of nearly $82 million dollars by several Indian tribes lobbying for favorable gaming legislation.[11]

Lobbying is extrapolitical in the sense that the special interests exerting pressure on lawmakers are not necessarily allied with any political party. In many cases, influence is sought wherever and with whomever can best accomplish the goals of lobbyists' clients. Democrat or Republican matters little, and both parties are culpable. Campaign contributions are often a vehicle for buying influence and are usually made irrespective of party affiliation. Such contributions, especially those that originate from large business concerns, are often made universally to all candidates for a given office, presumably facilitating access to the winner by the contributors or their representative lobbyists.

And it keeps getting worse. The term *revolving door* commonly refers to the transition from public service to the private sector and vice versa. In this potentially corrupting relationship, many government regulatory officials, upon leaving public office, are hired to represent the very firms they once regulated, or in the reverse case, ex-employees of regulated industries are appointed to key regulatory positions in government. This common practice seems like leaving the fox to guard the henhouse; it's simply not a good idea, for the hens anyway. Even though there are rules for government officials to ensure ethical conduct and avoidance of any conflict of interest, proving impropriety is not a clear or easy task. When George W. Bush took office, his administration recruited thirty-two executives from the weapons industry for appointments to policy-making positions in the Pentagon, National Security Council, the Department of Energy, and the State Department. By 2003, military contracts with the top ten Pentagon contractors had increased more than 75 percent.[12] Is this impropriety, or just beefed up national security? In a scandal uncovered by Senator John McCain, Darlene Druyun, an air force negotiator for weapons procurement, was sentenced to jail for approving close to $30 billon dollars in contracts to Boeing at the same time she negotiated lucrative jobs with Boeing for her daughter, her son-in-law, and finally herself.[13]

This "revolving door" has been used by industries in the environmental sector as well. At this writing, Gale Ann Norton, former secretary of the Department of the Interior is under investigation by the U.S. Justice Department to evaluate potential wrongdoing in her decision to award three oil shale leases on federal land, valued into the hundreds of billions of dollars, to Royal Dutch Shell PLC. Norton went to work for Royal Dutch Shell PLC in 2006, shortly after resigning her position as interior secretary.[14]

Soon after being sworn in, President Obama signed a new executive order aimed at regulating and reducing revolving door practices. Some question now exists as to whether the Obama administration is obeying its own regulation, as it has hired ex-lobbyists to fill policy-making positions on several occasions.[15] Whether or not the new executive order will make a difference in revolving door practices has yet to be seen. It seems clear, however, that the practice is probably unsound, and that the people, regardless of political or religious leanings, are being shortchanged as a result.

It seems there are two ways to progress. Either comprehensively regulate lobbying, which has been attempted in the past, or find ways to get more lobbyists to work for environmental goals. We favor regulation but, admittedly, past regulatory efforts have fallen short of their intended purpose and sometimes border on the ridiculous. Some of our "favorite" regulatory examples include the "toothpick rule," which permits lobbyists to serve food to lawmakers as long as it is eaten with a toothpick; the "gravy rule," which forbids lobbyists to serve food with gravy to public servants, as it could necessitate the use of utensils and therefore be considered a meal; and the "bagel rule," which states that serving bagels to lawmakers is fine as long as they are not topped with something expensive like lox or caviar. According to a 1996 House regulation, lobbyists can buy dinner for lawmakers only if it is a "widely attended event"— that is, attended by more than twenty-five people. That, in the scope of the regulations, is OK, because a lobbyist would have a hard time monopolizing a senator's time in a crowd.[16] But loopholes remain rampant, and lobbyists still persist as a major influence on governments worldwide.

If lobbyists can't be beaten, perhaps they can joined. If environmentally active citizens understand how lobbyists work, they might work through K Street channels as well, in greater numbers, to reduce environmental degradation and shape legislation beneficial to the environment. Ideally the changes being lobbied for will be scientifically defensible. Some such lobbyists already exist.

The Union of Concerned Scientists is an organization that lobbies for scientific integrity in policy making (see www.ucsusa. org). The organization got its start in 1969 at the Massachusetts Institute of Technology as a group of faculty and students opposed to the militarization of scientific research and proliferation of nuclear power. The group was an early leader in both the environmental movement and the arms control movement. For forty years, they've generated consequential documents that have helped shape legislation in a number of different areas, ranging from the 1972 United States–Soviet antiballistic missile treaty to recent California legislation curbing greenhouse gas emissions. We support public interest lobbies like the Union of Concerned Scientists and believe that such "open and accessible" lobbying is a beast quite different from the private and profit-driven lobbying that characterizes industrial lobbyists. Environmentally active citizens must recognize this important difference, so environmental educators ought to teach it.

Here again, we reiterate that the distortion of democracy represented by industrial lobbyists and special interest groups crosses political and social boundaries. Citizens of all races and creeds, politically right- or left-leaning, rich or poor, have the same right to live in an environment that is not toxic or threatening to present or future generations. Environmental education should attempt to bring people together under this maxim and make clear to our politicians that the environment belongs to all people, not to special interests or powerful conglomerates. Once that's accomplished, we can all happily return to hashing out the political particulars of our respective social structures.

For a more practical understanding of how the sorry state of world politics affects each and every one of us equally, let's examine what happened at COP15—the United Nations Climate Change Conference of 2009.[17] This globally attended summit conference was convened to discuss international solutions to climate change and its effects. In the months leading up to COP15, it seemed that world leaders (and their peoples) had finally begun to accept the scientific realities and predictions of impending environmental catastrophe and were multilaterally committed to negotiating a binding international treaty to reduce greenhouse emissions through a variety of verifiable methods. But that is not what happened.

The bias of governments toward economic development once again took precedence over the well-being of their peoples, and no binding treaty was signed or even proposed. Instead, a last-minute "accord" was agreed to, but it was not legally binding, lacked specific reduction targets, and had little architecture for making real impacts. This, however, did not stop the proponents of the accord from using adjectives like "milestone, landmark, and ground-breaking" to describe what many believe was the utter failure of global political leaders to effect meaningful change. If world citizens understood, via environmental education, more about the political mechanics of why our leaders seemingly ignore the urgency of climate change in favor of preserving industrial power, people might hold their leaders accountable, and we might not have to listen to their insulting rhetoric.

If the ticking clock of environmental degradation were superimposed over our political and legislative processes, it would be clear the latter is not keeping pace with the former. This means that our legislators, special interest lobbyists, industrial representatives, and the like can't really be trusted to act in the best interests of the people. Perhaps this is because their hands are tied by the lack of consensus resulting from the various perceptions of the problems at hand. Perhaps it's because legislators are generally out of office by the time the long-term implications of their decisions kick in. Perhaps it's because they just don't answer to the people anymore. But if the people act in decisive ways—by "voting" with their spending habits (buying sustainable products over those with greater environmental impacts) and letting leaders know through social networks and other channels that failure to act will cost them votes—we can jump-start timely, measurable, and effective action. So, who can do this? Teachers, religious leaders, parents, students, media representatives, business leaders . . . in short, all of us.

We have talked much about grassroots efforts as an effective means of bringing about broad-scale political awareness that can lead to change. Whether we all choose to exercise it or not, we, the people hold the power to change the world. We all need to know how our respective governments function. We all need to vote our consciences and effectively communicate our beliefs to others, as active citizens in a fluid community. We all need to develop the capacity to listen, discuss, and compromise, because that is what community means. But voting and learning might not be enough to move us collectively toward mitigation of the environmental consequences we may soon face. Social undercurrents, or what might be called a collective will, can spread virally and develop such momentum that they topple political regimes or overturn unassailable policies. The beginnings of such social galvanization can be quiet, can sometimes even be unknown to those who try hardest to bring it about. This is the phenomenon Daniel Goleman refers to when he talks about how the rules of the swarm might lead us to better our conditions even if, as individuals, we do not have, or grasp, a "master plan."[18] This is the power of a social groundswell brought about through individual efforts on a grassroots level. What follows are some examples of what we mean.

On January 27, 1973, the signing of the Paris Peace Accords ended U.S. military involvement in the Vietnam War. More than fifty-eight thousand Americans died during the conflict that also claimed the lives of millions of North and South Vietnamese soldiers and civilians. The involvement of the United States spanned six presidencies. In 1964, the Gulf of Tonkin Resolution provided President Lyndon Johnson with the power to escalate U.S. involvement without a formal declaration of war. Under Johnson, American troop presence in Vietnam surged from sixteen thousand to nearly five hundred thousand and was accompanied by an aggressive bombing campaign that lasted for more than three and a half years.

American opinion polls at the outset of the escalation in 1965 showed that more than 60 percent of the American public supported increased U.S. intervention. Opposition to the war was considered un-American. By 1971, however, public support had fallen to less than 28 percent,[19] even though America's leaders were still supporting the war effort. How did this occur? Antiwar sentiment traveled virally among a constantly growing percentage of the population. By the end of 1965, more than 35,000 young American men were being conscripted each month into military service,[20] and resistance to the draft was growing substantially, especially among students. Colleges all over America were fast becoming the staging ground for teach-ins and rallies that, in turn, spurred media interest. Uncensored news coverage from reporters on the front lines, daily tallies of war casualties and wounded, and images of the flag-draped coffins of dead American soldiers were becoming an everyday occurrence on the six o'clock news, and the antiwar movement grew stronger and stronger, spreading across political divides. Antiwar demonstrations spread throughout the world, often attended by hundreds of thousands of citizens. A majority of Americans were coming to believe the war they had initially supported was an unwinnable and brutal waste of American and Vietnamese lives. In 1971, the top-secret Pentagon Papers, leaked by a State Department official, detailed the series of high-level mistakes made by the government in determining Vietnam policy, including obfuscations associated with the passing of the Gulf of Tonkin resolution. Attempts by President Richard Nixon to suppress the Pentagon Papers eventually led to the Watergate investigations and his resignation in 1973. By the time the Pentagon Papers became public, it was clear that the American people wanted an end to the Vietnam War, and they were letting their politicians know it. People, working and thinking collectively, changed the course of political policy.

Freon, a chlorofluorocarbon (CFC), was a revolutionary discovery in 1928. It made refrigeration safer, led to the widespread adoption of domestic refrigeration, set the stage for the rapid growth of agribusiness, and brought new levels of comfort to people all over the world. It wasn't until the 1970s that two atmospheric chemists, F. Sherwood Rowland and Mario Molina, discovered that CFCs were degraded by ultraviolet radiation in the stratosphere, releasing chlorine. And this stratospheric chlorine destroyed ozone. Ozone is the atmospheric chemical that protects the surface of the earth from dangerous UV-B radiation. The stratospheric accumulation of ozone served as an important precursor to the colonization of land by marine organisms more than 500 million years ago.

Rowland and Molina realized that their discovery had important implications for human health and the health of the global environment. UV-B radiation causes skin cancers and cataracts and can damage plants and animals. The two men published their results in 1974,[21] a time when CFCs were widely used in refrigeration and plastics and as aerosol propellants. Four years later, CFCs were banned by the Environmental Protection

Agency for use in aerosols, over the objections of the international chemical industry, which questioned the validity of the findings. At that time only five countries agreed to ban CFCs, while others, concerned with adverse economic impacts, either agreed to small reductions or did little to reduce production. The problem of CFCs came to public attention in the mid-1980s, when British scientists discovered a continent-sized hole in the ozone layer. Their data showed rapid deterioration of atmospheric ozone, but the controversy over the Antarctic ozone layer remained until 1986, when the role of CFCs in ozone depletion was validated. The threat of skin cancer and other impacts to human health was no longer just theory, it was real and happening. In 1987, 27 nations signed the Montreal Protocol on Substances That Deplete the Ozone Layer,[22] the first ever global treaty to address climate problems. The protocol mandated a phase-out of CFCs throughout the world. Today, more than 196 countries have signed the protocol,[23] making it one of the most successful international efforts, and proving that such a collaboration is indeed possible. By all measures, this was a remarkably rapid call to arms that effectively addressed a globally threatening problem.

One defining feature of the CFC problem is that it was relatively easily addressed. Paul and Anne Ehrlich argued in their book *The Dominant Animal* that, unlike greenhouse gasses, CFCs were readily replaced with other chemicals (unfortunately, some of these replacements are greenhouse gases!).[24] Thus, public interest lobbies were effective at creating the political will to solve the problem. It was the ease of solving the problem, coupled with scientific consensus and public awareness, that led to rapid, widespread acceptance of the Montreal Protocol.

The Green Belt Movement (GBM) is a nongovernmental organization based in Kenya. It was founded in 1977 by political activist and environmentalist Wangari Maathai to "advocate for human rights and support good governance and peaceful democratic change through the protection of the environment."[25] Maathai believes that "the planting of trees is the planting of ideas,"[26] and following this simple axiom the GBM has engaged groups of Kenyan women to plant trees to prevent erosion and combat deforestation on a local scale. The GBM provides a support structure for the formation of community groups, helping them to establish nurseries for seedlings, then helps distribute seedlings to local farmers, who plant and care for the trees under the supervision of the groups. Initially, the GBM paid the groups a token sum for successfully planted seedlings on private land, but as the program grew they encouraged the groups to commercialize their nurseries, bringing money and jobs into their respective areas. At present, there are more than four thousand GBM groups in Kenya, 70 percent of whose members are women. By planting more than 30 million trees, tens of thousands of women have become more politically engaged, effecting a continuing contribution to global environmental conservation and bringing new skills hope to their communities.

In recent years, the focus of the GBM has shifted to the conservation of public, rather than private, lands. With the help of the United Nations Environment Programme, GBM founded the Pan-African Green Network, which is spreading GBM methodologies of social action and environmental conservation through Africa. Such community-based development has proven an effective grassroots method of environmental education that helps mobilize people to protect their resources.

The GBM has grown from simple tree planting to water management, to increasing food security by encouraging people to plant indigenous foods that grow well in the local environment, to advocating human rights, to fighting corruption and the illegal allocation of public lands, to providing HIV/AIDS education and prevention, and to facilitating pan-African sustainable development. From a humble start, the GBM has supplied a working example of how people, even those with few resources, working locally, can become an effective and powerful force for environmental change.

For motivated citizens to have a fighting chance of successes in grassroots endeavors, some knowledge of the dark underbelly of political process is probably necessary. In the following account, we describe some tactics used in political fights not because we believe the tactics are good ones or worth using, but because they are systematically brought to bear against any promising efforts to wrest power away from industry or impose social accountability.

Large and powerful companies in regulated businesses like tobacco, oil, and pharmaceuticals often hire consulting firms specializing in what is called "product defense" to assist them in fighting regulation. Such regulation could, among other things, remove dangerous products from the marketplace or inhibit industrial development for environmental reasons. This peculiar sector of the public relations world is what David Michaels calls "the manufacture of doubt" in his excellent 2008 book, *Doubt Is Their Product*.[27] Hill & Knowlton, one of the most experienced PR firms in the doubt industry, advertises on its Web site: "We build up a clear picture of what you want to achieve. Then put in place whatever is needed to get that result. Your success."[28] To accomplish that goal (which sounds a bit ominous to us), firms like Hill & Knowlton use a sophisticated set of tools to influence public opinion, which in turn pressures political representatives. This, coupled with the best efforts of industry lobbyists, often works remarkably well.

What we like to call the deliberate assassination of environmental facts by PR firms is accomplished by means of a tool kit that includes employing "expert" scientists to issue public announcements casting doubt on generally accepted scientific opinion, citing research that is not subject to the peer-review process or is simply false, publicly disseminating the message that regulation is driven by fanatical "tree-hugging" environmentalists, and waging PR campaigns to inform the public of the alleged dire economic consequences of regulation. These tactics create an undercurrent of public doubt because it is simply too difficult for an average person to determine where the truth really lies. This is greatly exacerbated by public education systems that fail to teach critical thinking.

In the last few months of 2009, public opinion in the United States made an about-face. A midyear poll showed that 65 percent of Americans believed global warming is a serious problem, compared to only 17 percent who thought no problem exists. Further, 88 percent believed the United States should either collaborate with other countries or set its own standards to address global climate change.[29] By the end of the same year, those percentages were changing fast, and the number of Americans who believed solid evidence exists for anthropogenic warming was decreasing.[30] Some of the change might be explained by prevailing global economic crises, which tend to refocus public concern on things economic. But a major reason for this turnaround in opinion is probably the organized attempts at discrediting accepted, peer-reviewed scientific opinion. This culminated in what pundits called "Climategate," which occurred when ten years of e-mail communications between various climate scientists were stolen and made public. What followed was a free-for-all public distortion of personal correspondence, often taken out of context, with the clear intent of undermining public confidence in the scientific basis for anthropogenic global warming. Unfortunately for all of us, it worked fairly well, and the result has been a large step backward for humankind. This reinforces the necessity of teaching an expanded and comprehensive civics to current and future generations, so that citizens understand how governments and special interests can manipulate public opinion to weaken regulatory outcomes.

Politics are everywhere; it's a fact of life. Some political systems are closed and corrupt, and others are open and transparent, but wherever and whatever they are, they define our ways of life. It is critical to the environmental stability of our planet, and perhaps to the future of the human species as well, that people understand the ins and outs of the political system under which they live. It is an essential step toward finding ways to initiate change either from within or outside the system, or both.

CHAPTER EIGHT

Consumption, Conservation, and Change

Our societies are driven by consumption, at least in the developed and developing world. Those with the wherewithal to acquire stuff do so, and those without can't wait to get developed so they can get stuff too. The more wherewithal people have, the more stuff they seem to want or need. Over the last several decades, America has witnessed a trend of extreme consumerism. In order to "keep up with the Joneses," typical American families of the middle class and up seem to want homes that are five thousand square feet or larger, multiple SUVs, oversize plasma screen televisions in every room, the newest Wii, the newest laptop computer, video iPods or the like, and the coolest cell phones. They also want personal watercraft, recreational vehicles, expensive exercise gear, Ugg boots, home cappuccino makers, double-door refrigerators with built-in juice dispensers, Harley-Davidson motorcycles—and the list goes on and on and on. And all this barely scratches the surface of what we Americans think is essential to our comfort and well-being. We deserve it, we work hard, and we have the right to enjoy the fruits of our labor. Don't we?

Our taste for new things keeps growing, and product cycles continue to decrease in length, and that is *very* good for global business. An example of this phenomenon is how quickly the DVD became widely accepted, compared to the time it took for the VCR to become commonplace. Another is how quickly our tastes changed in favor of flat screen televisions and monitors over those clumsy cathode tube predecessors (which, incidentally, use less energy). Such rapid shifts in the normative technology translate into the manufacture, transport, and disposal of far more stuff. Old products are cast aside in favor of this year's model, often with little or no regard for their fate. Technology has been good for creating toxic landfills full of dismantled personal electronics. Consider the average useful life of cellular phones, personal digital assistants, and laptop computers. Because of obsolescence and breakage, it is highly unusual for these products to remain in use for more than two to three years. And if they do last longer, it is not without new batteries, software, or firmware changes or updates.[1] Old technology tends to quickly lose all value; contrast the value of an antique rocking chair with that of an "antique" computer.

Why wouldn't we all want these new things? Just take a look around. Our societies are programmed to consume, and it starts when we are born. Many of us begin our lives watching television peppered with ads specifically targeted at children. They show us what games or toys we need or what kind of food we ought to eat. We, in turn, tell our parents, and they go out and get it for us. As we get older, our televisions, movies, magazines, and billboard advertisements reveal to us the worlds of beautiful, well-proportioned, and stylishly dressed people living in nicely furnished homes and driving expensive, intriguing automobiles with GPS touch screens. All stimuli direct us toward this modeled world, and so we do what we are taught and told: we consume.

Such consumption, while arguably good from a short-term economic perspective, is moving us rapidly toward a long-term ecological and environmental train wreck. And, shockingly, because ecological and environmental responses are likely to be nonlinear, the time and place of the particular tipping point that will bring disastrous global consequences are not known to us. The *Stern Review* has shown us that we actually can do something to avoid the worst outcomes, but it will cost much less in money, biodiversity, and human suffering if we do it now rather than later.[2] Those in developed countries must cut back, and those in the developing world should to heed our mistakes and not repeat them.

Environmental education can play a primary role in helping people learn why and how to change their behavior to reduce anthropogenic impacts on our planet. But simply teaching environmental topics will have little value if our societies continue to go about business as usual. We must teach a new message: that consumption has consequences for humanity's future. We must use less of everything and find ways to get more out what we do use. Achieving this is not at all easy and will probably require those living in developed countries to simply use less. Educational institutions would serve humanity well by teaching that it is each of our responsibility, as world citizens, to initiate and embrace conservation-minded legislation, which may deprive us of some of the goods and services we previously enjoyed.

How do we get from the consumerist mentality spreading across the planet, to a new way of thinking and behaving that promotes global sustainability? What is the first step? Assuming we are ready to conserve, what products or services ought we to cut? To answer these and other questions, some tools that help define what "consumption" and "impact" actually represent might be helpful.

What is human impact and how can we measure it? We might focus on air quality or water quality. We might focus on the number of species gone extinct or the surface area of our planet that has been paved over or otherwise developed. Biologist Jay Anderson notes that naturalness could be quantified by the amount of anthropogenic energy put into a system.[3] A paved road is less natural than a dirt road, which is less natural than a footpath. Since the industrial revolution, by most measures, humans have done a pretty good job of changing the face of the earth, making it less natural. We must push past assessment and define human impact in a way that helps us identify possible solutions.

Our human ecosystems are made up of basic elements like population, social organization, technology, and environment, each of which interacts with each other. These complex interactions determine the magnitude of environmental impacts of human societies. Modeling and examining these linkages can offer valuable insights into how impacts occur and provide a tool kit helpful in projecting and understanding future impacts.

In 1971, Paul Ehrlich and John Holdren developed the I=PAT equation (impact = population × affluence × technology).[4] Using this equation, we can see that a country with a large population that is affluent, that consumes a lot of sophisticated widgets that, in turn, require energy to manufacture or maintain, will have a much larger impact than a country of even more numerous subsistence farmers who, by comparison, consume much less because they cannot afford such energy-consuming technology. The I=PAT equation came under fire for being simplistic and not necessarily diagnostic. One criticism on the dimensionality of I=PAT came from biologist Barry Commoner, who focused on negative technological developments. He believed these were primarily to blame for environmental degradation, unlike Ehrlich, who believed the population was the primary issue.[5]

Time passed and I=PAT evolved. A modification of I=PAT, called ImPACT, was proposed in 2002 by Paul Waggoner and Jesse Ausubel. ImPACT sought to provide a tool for analyzing the inherent sustainability of an ecosystem by quantifying the "component forces of environmental impact" and the "actors" that drive and influence them.[6] With ImPACT, specific actors can be targeted to change specific causes. In this modification, impact (Im) is a function of: population size (P), income/affluence (A), consumer behavior (C), and the production efficiency of goods (T). To reduce impact, it's possible to target parents in order to reduce birthrate (P); worker behavior influences per capita GDP (A); consumers might reduce the intensity of use through conservation (C); and the producers might invent more efficient technology to increase production efficiency (T). Each of these can be used to define a set of specific challenges.

Yet another variation, STIRPAT, which is an acronym for stochastic impacts by regression on population, affluence, and technology, is the brainchild of sociologists Thomas Dietz, Eugene Rosa, and Richard York.[7] This new equation addresses the problem that human systems rarely behave with the mathematical uniformity found in nonhuman systems. Neither I=PAT nor ImPACT allows for random variables, but STIRPAT, which adheres to interdisciplinary analyses, integrates them into the equation, rendering a more detailed quantification of anthropogenic impacts.[8]

I=PAT, ImPACT, and STIRPAT are useful because they help us focus on the complex relationships that make up environmental impacts. But we must remember that models are just that; they are crude approximations of reality. Biologist Richard Levins wrote that mathematical models, in order to facilitate our understanding, prediction, and modification of nature, must maximize generality, precision, and realism, but this, he concluded, can't be done. Consequently, Levins stated, generality must be sacrificed in favor of realism and precision, or realism must be sacrificed in favor of generality and precision, or precision must be sacrificed for generality and realism.[9] Yet, if I=PAT, STIRPAT, and ImPACT models are viewed as heuristic tools rather than precise predictive equations, they offer powerful ways to shape how we think about our ecological footprint and clarify what *impact* actually means.

Armed with these analytic tools, where should we ask environmental education to go from here? In an effort to teach how to solve a problem, we must define the problem. So let's look at population, for example. Is it the key problem as Ehrlich and Holdren thought? In 1968, Paul Ehrlich wrote *The Population Bomb*, in which he argued there would be mass starvation in coming decades as humanity overused its resources and agriculture failed to keep pace with population growth.[10] Ehrlich argued that from a humanistic and ecological perspective it was essential to reduce the rate of population growth. While starvation and chronic malnutrition are still global problems, the catastrophic population collapse that Ehrlich predicted has not come to pass. This may have been primarily the result of the green revolution in agriculture, which we mentioned in chapter 1. But the population catastrophe that Ehrlich predicted may have been simply delayed by advances in technology, advances that, in themselves, have brought about grave and unforeseen environmental consequences. Clearly, if we want to reduce deleterious ecological impacts and increase the quality of life, we should think about reducing global population. But this reduction can potentially become barbaric unless it is addressed purely and solely through an educational approach. Teaching ourselves that life can be easier for individuals and families when some thought is given to planned parenthood might be a good place to start.

The effect of increased population is multiplied by various types of impacts. These impacts may be enhanced or mitigated by technology. In the context of individual environmental impact, our analytical tools reveal that one person in say, Bangladesh, is probably not equivalent to one person in the United States. This is the basis for much of the current disagreement between countries when it comes to developing an international protocol to address global warming. Many developing nations point out that, while their populations might be large, their people are poor and therefore use fewer resources than in developed countries, entitling them to fewer restrictions on industrial emissions than more affluent nations. They draw attention to the fact that the United States and other developed countries use the vast majority of the world's resources. For instance, if we look at per capita energy consumption in 2005, according to the World Resources Institute Earth Trends data portal, each person in Bangladesh used 171 kilograms of oil equivalent (koe), while each United States citizen used 7,885.9 koe, and citizens of Qatar topped the list at 19,466 koe.[11] Now, let's do some math. According to United Nations data, there were about 142 million people in Bangladesh in 2005 (a poor and "overpopulated" country by most standards) and a mere 813,000 in Qatar.[12] This means that Bangladesh's total energy consumption was 24.282 billion koe, while tiny Qatar, used a total of 15.83 billion koe. What about the United States? According to the U.S. Census Bureau, the 2005 population was 295,560,549.[13] This means that Americans used a total of 2,330,760,933,359 koe. Yes, you read that correctly, 2.3 trillion koe. Framed this way, is population the problem? It's certainly part of the problem, and we would all benefit from reducing it, but the real issue is per capita energy use. Some people use more energy than others, and it's those people who "count more" in this discussion, because they have a larger ecological impact. They are the ones who must act sooner and more decisively than those with lower per capita consumption rates.

Energy consumption seems an excellent way to measure impact, for the following reasons. First, most of the world's energy comes from oil, natural gas, and coal. In America, these sources account for around 85 percent of our total energy production.[14] Global transportation infrastructure as well is almost entirely powered by fossil fuels, which create greenhouse gasses that threaten our collective future. Second, energy consumption focuses on something that is under both the individual's and the country's control. Individuals can conserve energy, and nations can offer incentives, which might include the development of renewable sources of energy, energy efficient building practices and materials, and development and implementation of energy efficient means of transportation.

For argument's sake, let's compare energy consumption to greenhouse gas production as another possible metric. Carbon dioxide is the greenhouse gas primarily responsible for the atmospheric warming that the earth is experiencing. And there are other dangerous greenhouse gases, like methane, to think about. We already know methane is a particularly scary one because it traps more than twenty times more heat than CO_2 does. Focusing on greenhouse gas production originating from political units like countries or states misses the important point that, even if these formerly contained methane sinks fall within the geographical boundaries of a given country, the release of the methane gas may be driven by carbon use in more industrialized nations.

If we accept per capita energy consumption as our primary indicator of human impact, what role might environmental education play in helping to reduce it? The details probably vary according to location. Educational efforts everywhere must build a foundation of individual responsibility and environmental awareness through social engagement. However, emphasizing development and implementation of sustainable infrastructure may yield greater short-term benefits in developing nations, whereas teaching people how to reduce consumption might pay off more quickly in developed countries. Either way, if we continue our rush toward global development and "free market" economies, we are going to have to find a better and more sustainable way of doing things, or we will eventually industrialize ourselves to an economic and ecological collapse.

Environmental education should take the lead in stimulating interest in new ways of developing our world.

What about technology? In numerous instances technology has come to humanity's rescue, providing unforeseen, sometimes unimagined solutions to grave problems facing the world. Consider the green revolution. Can society expect technology, once again, to rise to the occasion and relegate the potential threat of global warming to yesterday's news? Our governments would like us to think so. Industry would certainly like us to think so, as corporations stand to directly profit from technological solutions. And perhaps it will come to pass, as they would have us believe. It would certainly make life easier for all of us. But we ought not to depend on "eleventh hour" technological solutions to global warming.

This is not to say, however, that technology can't help us out of our predicament. Technological advancement plays, and will play, a central part in helping us reduce our dependence on fossil fuels, but we must work diligently to improve technology to help us slow the rate of ecological destruction and find sustainable ways to live and prosper. Technological advances are needed in transportation, energy usage, construction, energy production, agriculture, and natural resource use.

We must increase the fuel efficiency of our vehicles, which might entail reviewing or enacting legislation like the U.S. corporate average fuel economy, or CAFE, standards for fuel efficiency, or providing public (and private) incentives for the design and manufacture of high-mileage cars. The Automotive X Prize, a $10 million dollar prize to the team that designs and builds the best one-hundred-mile-per-gallon, production-ready automobile, is one good example.[15]

New buildings and building materials can be designed with energy efficiency and conservation in mind to minimize environmental impacts. Establishing new building standards, like the Leadership in Energy and Environmental Design (LEED) certification, may encourage sustainable construction through a "whole-building" approach.[16] The LEED certification adheres to a set of green building practices and parameters that include sustainable site selection, water efficiency, energy conservation, sustainable materials use, indoor environmental quality, and innovation in design. There is also an important educational component to the LEED program that helps owners, builders, tenants, and managers learn how to get the most out of the green systems inherent in LEED-certified projects. The Natural Resources Defense Council takes the process a step further by teaching people involved with LEED how to spread the word about sustainable building by contacting local media and involving their respective communities.[17]

One beneficial side effect of revolutionizing current construction practices and materials is that it provides opportunities to rethink how the physical environment shapes the way we think about our world and how we fit into it. If we work to create building designs and supporting technologies that both respect and reflect the ecological aspects of a given area, we can build living and working spaces that blend form, function, and landscape, instead of industrial parks, housing developments, and commercial malls that tend to further isolate us from the natural world.

Creating new sources of power from renewable resources will do much to reduce greenhouse gases, and every cent invested in such technology by governments, individuals, and the private sector is probably money well spent. Advances in wind power and solar energy technology already offer a low-impact alternative to fossil fuels. New energy technologies hold promise, not only as possible solutions to our environmental woes, but for future economic prosperity as well.

But technology is not the only answer, and we should never forget that it was technology that got us all into this mess in the first place. Today, there is a tendency to think of any technological advancement as a good thing (newer, faster computers and the like). This kind of thinking is flawed because it is based on a philosophy of economic growth above all else, where more and faster is always better.

In any discussion of improving efficiency through technology, a casual mention of the Jevons Paradox is worthwhile. In 1866, economist William Stanley Jevons wrote *The Coal Question*, in which he pointed out that any technological breakthroughs that increase the efficiency by which a resource is used tend to cause an increase in consumption, rather than a decrease.[18] Increased efficiency can lead to decreased cost of a resource, thereby increasing demand. For example, if the cost of gasoline goes down, people tend to drive faster or take longer trips, because they can more readily afford to do so. Automobile accidents didn't decline after the introduction of antilock brakes; people drove faster in bad conditions. So, when we look to technology to help us get more from less, we must also make sure that we understand, as individuals, the value to the community of choosing not to throw away any potential gains.

In developing new things, we rarely ask ourselves what problems might be caused by a new technology, or if there exists some problem that this emerging technology really must address. Additionally, when we evaluate emerging technology, we must keep the precautionary principle in mind. The precautionary principle, as applied to the environment, states that, where action or policy creates the potential for harming the environment, but scientific consensus or conclusive evidence of this does not exist, caution must be exercised in all phases of implementation; and the burden of proving there are no likely deleterious consequences rests with the advocates of that action or policy.[19]

As climate change has gained more credibility with governments and the public in recent years, our leaders have increasingly spoken of future investment in alternative energy sources, renewable energy, clean coal technology, oil extraction from tar sands, biofuels, and more. These things are touted as a kind of "new economic revolution" comprising vast opportunities for future growth. We hope to reduce greenhouse gas emissions in the future by working to create alternative sources of energy. We are oriented, by such rhetoric, toward believing that change will take place sometime in the future. No political or business leader publicly advocates cutting back on energy use or using already existing technologies to promote conservation today. It seems we are conveniently missing a very important fact: that we already have the means to immediately reduce impacts. Conservation is the first and easiest way.

Let's start with public transportation by making it more attractive in places where it isn't, and more efficient in places where it already exists. New technology can and will be helpful in accomplishing this, but we don't have to wait for it before we begin building better public transportation infrastructures. Buses and trains are not the ultimate answer, as they are mostly fossil fuel dependant, but in the short term we can live with solutions that produce more than zero emissions if we realize net gains from reducing the number of cars on the road. We might legislate "mass-transit only" lanes on routes into and out of our major cities during peak traffic hours, or provide remote suburban parking areas and restrict private automobile access to downtown areas to facilitate increased public transportation use. Both light and heavy rail systems work well for medium- and longer-distance travel, producing far less pollution and far fewer greenhouse gases than airplanes do. In some areas, we may benefit from removing municipal transportation authorities' monopoly on transporting people around and create private shuttles that can quickly adapt to people's needs while reducing the number of vehicles in urban areas. Tax incentives for using public transportation, and government incentives to businesses that provide it, might also help get things quickly moving in a greener direction. Carpool lanes work well, so let's raise the minimum number of riders per car to further encourage ride sharing. If we make short-term sacrifices like these, we can substantially slow greenhouse gas emissions now. These are some things that car-dependent cultures might want to consider, and which educational institutions in those same cultures might want to introduce in class discussions.

Increasing the efficiency of electrical appliances can lead to immediate energy reductions, but, as we have already seen, the best technological intentions can sometimes have adverse effects. According to Lawrence Berkeley National Laboratory, an estimated 5 to 10 percent of home energy use goes to power devices on standby.[20] Simply turning off unused appliances can save substantially on household energy. One concrete measure to facilitate these easily gotten reductions would be to legislate a ban on manufacturing consumer products with the standby feature. Such a ban might be slightly inconvenient, but it seems a small sacrifice, given the returns. Many appliances and personal electronics use rechargeable built-in batteries to save "user settings" but better technologies like compact flash cards don't require any energy to save data and are already available. Simple things make a difference if enough of them are developed and widely implemented. For example, one easy way to save energy is to design Web pages to have black (i.e., pixels off) rather than white (i.e., pixels on) backgrounds. Blackle, a Google portal, does exactly this and has saved (at this writing) more than 2.1 million watt-hours since it appeared on the Internet.[21]

Obtaining our food from local, sustainable family farms can significantly reduce environmental impacts. Food distributed locally saves the fossil fuels consumed in transport, and farming techniques used by small farms are typically less consumptive then those of large-scale corporate farms. Communities benefit from small farms as revenues tend to stay in the community instead of being siphoned off to absentee owners, and more jobs are available because smaller farms depend less on heavy machinery. This is not only true for developed countries but has also proven to work well in developing nations of the third world.[22] And it requires only education to implement.

Local food production is not a substitute for energy efficiency. In some cases, it is more cost effective to ship products longer distances to markets, rather than growing them in energy intensive and unsustainable ways locally. For instance, eating New Zealand lamb in England uses less carbon overall than eating lamb grown in England because the costs of shipping do not outweigh the carbon savings of New Zealand green farming practices. The British supermarket Tesco began placing carbon labels on foods in 2008 so consumers would know the costs, both in money and environmental impacts, of what they purchase.[23]

Grass farming, a movement pioneered in New Zealand, yields a diversity of foods from "family scale" farms and requires active human management. Grass farming is based on moving livestock and other animals through endemic grass pastures in controlled ways that mimic natural grazing patterns. If animals eat too much in one area, their foraging reduces, rather than enhances productivity. This natural farming system produces healthy, resistant soil and sod, increases productivity per acre, and reduces overall farming costs.[24] When done carefully, grass farming has proven to enhance, rather than deplete, nutrients and produces more food per unit area per dollar than techniques employed on large industrial farms. If factory farms can be gradually abandoned in favor of localized grass farming, additional benefits will be realized from improved food quality and safety as well as from the conversion of corporate feedlots and feed-crop land to planted areas that help absorb atmospheric CO_2. Moreover, grass farming requires no new technology and can be implemented immediately.

Here is something else to consider: if we all cut back substantially on eating meat, the costs of mitigating climate change and stabilizing atmospheric CO_2 content at 450 parts per million can be radically reduced by up to $20 trillion dollars![25] Farming livestock requires a massive amount of energy. To produce a kilo of beef, cows must eat fifteen kilos of grain which, requires fertilizers, land, and energy to produce. Eliminating meat from our diets, or decreasing the amount we consume, will reduce methane and nitrous oxide emissions from livestock farming and free up vast amounts of farmland currently in use by the livestock industry. This land can then be converted to small farms employing more environmentally sustainable means of food production.[26] This is an informed choice each of us can make today that will start reducing impacts tomorrow. Again, no new technology needed, just education and a commitment to change.

Current evidence suggests that although we talk about cutting back on the stuff we use, for the sake of the greater good, we frequently don't follow through. We seem to be waiting for the technological breakthroughs that will allow us to go on as we have in the past. We don't want to give anything away, because we perceive our possessions and social status to be our absolute right. Many people think of the overall system in which we exist as economic, rather than ecological. They see our environment as made up of resource sectors waiting to be converted into wealth, apparently with no limits. But our economies cannot continue to grow forever. At some point we will run out of something; raw materials, labor, energy, space . . . something will give. One of the greatest challenges for environmental education is encouraging people to think about what the logical outcome of lives lived under these premises might be. In his book *The Long Emergency,* James Kunstler argues that a massive human catastrophe is just around the corner and will be precipitated when oil dries up.[27] Because our society depends so heavily on fossil fuels, it will be difficult or impossible to make replacement technology without reliable oil. He paints a compelling and shocking scenario, one we can work now to avoid. Educators will play a vital role in helping avoid ecological collapse and the "long emergency." One way educators can help accomplish this is to make people aware of where their stuff comes from and what will become of it when it is cast aside. They must teach us to use less and live closer to nature. They must teach us how cheap fossil fuels have led us down a scary path of self-destruction that even our best and brightest minds might not be able to get us out of if we don't move to address the problems now.

In this age of globalization, knowing what's involved in the production and disposal of consumables is a complicated matter. The consequences of consumption are not often visible, as the distances are often great between areas where resources are extracted and goods are produced, and where those same goods are consumed. In recent years, some innovative educational tools have emerged that make it easier to see these correlations. *The Story of Stuff,* a film produced exclusively for Internet distribution in 2007, does an excellent job of illustrating the limitations of a materials economy, while pointing the way toward new and sustainable practices and ways of thinking (see www.storyofstuff.com/index.php) This film, along with books like Fred Pearce's *Confessions of an Eco-Sinner,* provides the public with the complete picture of what goes into the products we take for granted.[28] Both unveil the true costs of our unbridled growth, not only in environmental terms, but in human ones as well. The underlying theme, however, is one of hope for the future, based on existing ingenuity and the intellectual capacity of the human species. Books and films like these help educators explain that there is much more to what we use than we are aware of, that an action as seemingly insignificant as, say, grocery shopping is not insignificant at all. Understanding this is a necessary step toward acting to change our consumption patterns in order to lessen environmental impacts and improve the global human condition.

Recycling is good, but it requires energy and other natural resources and often comes with a high cost. It's true that we can all benefit from recycling but we must be smart about it, and our governments must help make the transition to producing and using recycled goods cost-beneficial, safe, and attractive to business. This might come in the form of tax incentives or subsidies like those that many nations currently offer to unsustainable agribusiness. More uses and applications must be found for recycled materials, and this may require revamping accepted practices in industries like construction and manufacturing to integrate new, more sustainable materials into their products and services. Governmental support might also come in the form of laws protecting workers from the exploitive compensation levels and hazardous conditions prevalent in third world waste-processing and recycling plants, as developed nations, in a continuing quest for cheap goods and services, outsource their dirty work. Surely, the developed world would pay a few cents more per product to ensure a minimum standard of living for the people who make and dispose of the goods developed countries consume.

While recycling may be better than throwing things away, reusing and reducing are much more effective ways of helping the environment. In the summer, Dan lives and works in Gothic, Colorado, a former ghost town converted into a biological research station. The area is rich with low-priced thrift stores, and reusing things is a way of life there. The Gothic Exchange is a place where unwanted items are placed until somebody finds a new use for them. There is a lack of thrift in the developed world, probably driven by advertising and the desire to increase our social status, but it is not too late to begin squeezing more useful life out of the things we buy. Simply choosing not to replace the clothes we wear for additional year or two will bring significant reductions to environmental impacts. Our future will likely be brighter if we can relearn to value simpler pleasures rather than constantly looking toward our next purchase.

Developed countries must take additional responsibility for the current state of environmental affairs, as they are generally the ones that consume the most. Paradoxically, the most developed countries are often the places where the detrimental effects of growth are felt the least, leading to substantial resistance to the idea of cutting consumption patterns. If the conversion of resources is the basis of creature comforts, and resources are indeed finite, it would follow that the "quantity" of comfort is also finite in the world. Rich, developed countries will benefit by sharing with poorer nations some of the comfort they currently hoard and import. The rewards will come in the form of increased global political stability and cultivation of sustainable life-support systems, from which all countries benefit. If we expect a habitable planet in the near future, the thresholds of wealth and poverty will need some adjusting. Any hope for the global proliferation of equitable trade practices and safe working environments, which are also integral aspects of solving earth's environmental problems, will come most quickly through increased education in developed nations.

A healthy environment benefits us all. Clean air and water are necessary to the health and well-being of life on our planet and, as such, are a fundamental right. These are common things requiring common stewardship, protection, and management, and which transcend political, religious and economic boundaries. We must always remember that the earth is limited in its ability to support life. If it goes bad for one, it goes bad for all. An important and concise call to global action came in 1987 with the publication of *Our Common Future,* a summary report of the United Nations World Commission on Environment and Development also known as the Brundtland Report. The report urged international and multilateral efforts to combat environmental degradation, poverty, and the spread of conflict; promote food security and sustainable development; control population; and preserve biodiversity on earth. It suggested that a new era of cooperation would be necessary to protect and sustainably manage these common resources, which it described as "marked by a fundamental unity from which there is no escape."[29]

Certain important concepts and problems must be addressed in the management of common resources. Ecologist Garrett Hardin, in his landmark paper of 1968, identified one such problem, which he called "the tragedy of the commons."[30] Essentially, Hardin said that when common resources are open-access (shared equally by all), the benefits to an individual who "cheats"—by using more than a fair share of the resource—outweigh the costs to that individual. This leads to eventual overuse and to tragedy. He uses the example of a pasture where herdsmen maintain their flocks. Ideally, each flock should be equal in size so that each herdsman realizes the same benefit. If one herdsman decides to increase the size of his flock by one animal, the detriment of overgrazing is equally shared by all herdsmen, but the benefit from the sale of that additional animal goes only to the offending herdsman. Because of this, Hardin believed, the free and equal sharing of common resources is inherently doomed.

In the case of pollution, waste materials put into the ocean or the atmosphere (the commons) create detrimental impacts that are shared by all who use the oceans or breathe the air. The recent Deepwater Horizon blowout has revealed this all too well to those who rely on the Gulf of Mexico for food, jobs, and recreation. The cost borne by an individual who disposes of such waste into a common resource is less than the cost, to that individual, of cleaning up the mess. This, in part, is how we came to the environmental circumstances in which we find ourselves today.

Where does this leave us? True commons might be open-access things like the Internet or a body of knowledge, where one person's use does not detract from the use-value of another. What Hardin talked about are common-pool resources, where one person's use subtracts benefits from others. Is the decline of the commons really inevitable, as Hardin postulated? The answer is that there is no set answer. New research and resource management strategies have emerged indicating that, with proper structure, common-pool resources can be successfully managed for collective benefit. Cases like the lobster fishery in Maine, and the implementation of individual transferable quotas in New Zealand coastal fisheries, have proven successful in helping fishery stocks rebound to sustainable harvest levels.[31] Another recent study shows that when forest commons are owned and collectively managed by communities, rather than governments, deforestation actually decreases,[32] which not only goes against Hardin's predictions but also runs contrary to commonly accepted management policies. A key aspect of these successful strategies is they were generally developed in harmony with regional or local cultures, institutions, knowledge, and practices, rather than determined solely by absentee legislators as a national fix-all solution for diverse local problems. They depend on community awareness and involvement for their overall success, which depends on effective monitoring and enforcement and the prevention of "free riding."

Creating the atmosphere of cooperation that can flourish in our communities is a significant challenge to education, to government, and to the consumptive lifestyle that humanity currently embraces. Cooperation, as it turns out, is difficult to evolve and, once evolved, difficult to maintain, because cooperation, in an evolutionary sense, means helping someone out at a cost to oneself, and that may be contrary to our nature. But we are unique in our logical capacity to surmount what may be our self-destructive nature. Garrett Hardin believed in this capacity, and wrote that education can "counteract the natural tendency to do the wrong thing."[33]

We are capable of building on our insights and learning from our mistakes, but we must see ourselves as a part of a natural global community made up of diverse local groups, for which humans are the stewards, perhaps by default. The responsibility rests on each and every one of us. We already have many of the tools to aid us in the transition we collectively face; we just need to use them. And education is our best hope for solving our current environmental problems.

CHAPTER NINE

An Evolving Metric

In previous chapters, we've talked about what should be taught to create an environmentally aware, ecologically literate, and environmentally active population. We've talked about why this is essential, and we've outlined some of the obstacles that stand in the way of accomplishing the task. Let's assume, for a moment, that everyone agrees environmental education is important, and that its scope ought to be somewhere along the lines of what we have laid out so far. Let's further assume that grassroots efforts are successful in getting a foot in the door, and that environmental education, coupled with social involvement, finds its way into our schools to a significant degree. Does this mean we have been successful? If one approach works particularly well, how would we know it? If another approach doesn't really work at all in practice, but it is one we were convinced would be extremely effective, how might we see past our bias to the truth? Without proper evaluation, it is difficult to assert that a particular environmental education program (or any educational program) is effective.

Evaluation can reveal information essential to making sound decisions about many aspects of an intervention or curriculum. For instance, evaluation can help us quantify overall program performance, such as whether or not desired program goals have been achieved. Evaluation can help us determine funding needs, allocation priorities, and staffing requirements. And it can help us identify the effectiveness of teaching staff. Educational program evaluation is so important that many programs are designed around evaluation parameters and methods, and such evaluation is a necessary component of initial program approval or implementation. So, if meaningful evaluation is a time-tested and key part of education, why don't we know what works? Why are many schools failing to educate effectively? Why has educational reform been a hot topic of every incoming American political administration of the last half-century? Might this be some indication that currently accepted evaluation systems are flawed?

In this chapter, we attempt to identify some of these shortcomings and suggest alternative ideas and methods that can help with rethinking and reworking how educational programs are evaluated, and help achieve better success in these programs. Properly implementing an "evidence-based" evaluation approach can provide quantitative feedback on whether a given curriculum or intervention actually brings about the changes in behavior we believe environmental education must produce. Proper evaluation must be an inherent part of program design.

Evidence-based analysis has its roots in medical research, and to better explain how it works, we will use a medical analogy. Let's say your doctor tells you that your blood pressure is abnormally high and must be reduced. She tells you that to accomplish this reduction, you may have to take medication the rest of your life. You ask her about alternatives, and she suggests that trying 2.5 hours of aerobic exercise per week, coupled with a drastic reduction in your salt intake, might help reduce it naturally.[1] You decide to give this a try before committing yourself to a lifetime of medicine. How did she know that these activities may help reduce blood pressure? The short answer: randomized controlled trials and meta-analysis.

Randomized controlled trials are experiments conducted where a treatment is assigned randomly to a group of patients. For example, the first patient through the door with a particular symptom gets the therapeutic treatment, while the second patient is allocated to a placebo control treatment. In "double-blind" testing, neither the doctor nor the patient knows whether the treatment the patient receives is real or a placebo. Scientists try to eliminate bias through randomization. After all, you wouldn't want the doctor giving the new treatment to those who look relatively sicker, or saying, "We're doing this study, and I'm going to give you the drug that we know doesn't work"! To demonstrate effectiveness, a novel therapy should perform better than a placebo. In comparative-effectiveness research, new therapies are compared to older ones to determine whether the new therapy works as well as or better than the traditional approach.

But we've all heard about controversies over treatments. Some studies show that one treatment works, while others show that it does not. Does coffee lead to an increased risk of cancer or not? Does getting an MRI for lower back pain lead to better outcomes? Does exercise really reduce blood pressure, and if so, how much is needed? Are mammograms good or bad, and at what age should they be given? Which study should one believe?

Meta-analysis is a statistical tool that allows combining the results from a number of different studies to estimate the overall effect of a particular treatment. This tool was developed by Arizona State University professor Gene Glass in response to critical reviews written about psychotherapy. He singled out a particular set of reviews written by one critic, noting that they seemed arbitrary and idiosyncratic. In part, this was because the reviews in question did not consider non-peer-reviewed literature, studies without untreated control groups, or those the reviewer had deemed subjective or not significant. Glass realized that, to have a comprehensive understanding of a phenomenon, it was essential to use all of the data. Thus, as Glass says, by antithesis, systematic reviews and meta-analysis were born.[2]

A good systematic review finds all the studies that tested a general hypothesis (e.g., does exercise reduce resting blood pressure?). The statistical effect of each study is estimated and then combined in a weighted manner. Statistical effect size is a way to infer the magnitude of an intervention on an outcome variable. For instance, the effect of smoking one cigarette on longevity is much smaller than the effect of smoking two packs of cigarettes a day. There are different ways to calculate effect sizes, but the main point is that interventions or treatments with bigger effect sizes mean that the treatment has more effect on the outcome than those with smaller effect sizes. By "combined in a weighted manner," we mean simply that researchers have greater confidence in drawing a conclusion when they have more evidence to support it. Thus, studies with large sample sizes should have a greater impact on researchers' conclusions than studies with smaller sample sizes. A weighted average is calculated by summing the proportion of the total that a given study contributes to the overall data set multiplied by its effect.

Meta-analyses have another important feature: they allow evaluators to find groups of studies that have similar effects. For instance, what if we hypothetically find that smoking increases cancer rates for women but not for men? This would be an important finding. When conducting a meta-analysis, often the most interesting finding is not that there is an overall effect, or even the size of the effect, but that there are quantitatively different effects for different groups. These groups could be based on national origin, socioeconomic status, or even different interventions. By performing systematic reviews and meta-analyses, researchers can use evidence to help improve outcomes. This process not only helps evaluators employ interventions that work but may be used to discover cost-effectiveness as well.

It is not surprising that evidence-based approaches have found their way into fields other than medicine.[3] Glass himself is an educational psychologist and has been a strong proponent of systematic reviews in education. The fields of wildlife management and conservation biology often aim to conduct active adaptive management, whereby the outcomes of experiments are used to inform ongoing management decisions. And more recently, there has been a call for systematic reviews in conservation biology, in which management lore often builds up over years without proper evaluation (e.g., do hedgerows increase biodiversity? Do regular controlled burns reduce the chance of catastrophic fires? Does forest clear-cutting increase sediment flow into streams?).

Using the best evidence, it is possible to create a "decision tree analysis," which is a way to use information to help predict what the best treatment might be. In a medical application, this approach creates an "expert system" that helps clinicians make treatment decisions.[4] Using expert systems ensures that each potentially important symptom is recorded, and a comprehensive evaluation is typically required before making a diagnosis. Many believe this approach can help increase cures, reduce health care costs, and reduce mistakes by encouraging comprehensive examinations.

Unfortunately, in fields that purport to adopt these practices, we frequently find they are used improperly. These include the fields of health care, wildlife management, and conservation biology. In wildlife management, for instance, agencies sometimes talk about using adaptive management, but few really do. There are a number of reasons for this. When dealing with an endangered species, as an example, a proper control might require no action, and taking no action may be deemed unethical. We think the failure to adopt properly conceived evidence-based evaluation emerges from confusion about what evaluation really is, personal and institutional inflexibility, and an inability to identify the important questions that need evaluation.

How does all this fit into educational evaluation? Properly designed randomized and controlled studies in educational evaluation are rare. We find this puzzling, since each class may be viewed as an experimental unit. Understanding why properly randomized and controlled studies are rare will require an in-depth look at the nature of educational evaluation.

There are two complementary types of educational evaluation: formative and summative.[5] Formative evaluation, much like adaptive management, is evaluation designed to help improve the study or improve the efficacy of an intervention. Its main goal is to improve work in progress. Summative evaluation is typically retrospective and concerned with assessing achievements.

One important thing about formative evaluation is that, when it is done well, it involves stakeholders in the process. Stakeholders are those who have some concern or involvement in a program. This "buy-in" is important to any properly designed evaluation plan. It is now widely recognized in many fields that projects are more likely to fail if stakeholders are not integral in project design. Identifying exactly who the stakeholders really should be, however, requires some finesse. The current process tends to consider administrators, program designers, and funding agencies or grantors as primary stakeholders. Perhaps considering students, teachers, and possibly parents as primary stakeholders, instead of those whose concerns lie with aspects other than the quality of the educational experience (like costs or compliance), might prove more effective. This is especially true when environmental programs are designed, and expected, to change behaviors.

Another attribute of formative evaluation is that it may involve a variety of evaluation tools. While properly controlled studies with quantitative metrics of success could be an important part of such an evaluation, it is also essential to understand how stakeholders feel about the project. Thus, formative evaluation can improve the way curricula and interventions are presented by utilizing observations, interviews, focus groups, self-reporting forms, and other qualitative evaluation tools.

Ultimately it is essential to know what works and what doesn't. This is a role of summative evaluation, and this is one thing we think is inadequately done in educational evaluation. It is rare that summative evaluations use formal randomized control studies. Without the use of such controlled experiments, we believe, valuable opportunities to hone design and evaluate projects may be missed. To illustrate, let's say that each classroom could be considered an experimental unit. The key question is: does a particular program or intervention generate a desirable outcome? An experimental design that allows us to isolate the effect of what we want to measure requires a before-after, control-impact survey. Classes are randomly allocated to either an intervention or a control. Surveys conducted before the intervention or control procedure is implemented would measure what students know. After the intervention, another survey of both groups would be conducted. By comparing the difference after the treatment to before the treatment, in both the control and treatment groups, it's possible to isolate the effect of a treatment. To properly isolate the effect of a treatment, it is essential to control for development or ontogenetic changes that may have affected behavior, like other classes or interventions.

This simple design is powerful in many contexts, from assessing the effectiveness of blood pressure treatments in medicine to determining whether taking students on field trips to natural areas improves environmental awareness. But there are obstacles to implementation. The political will may not be there for instituting programs that systematically vary educational experiences to optimize outcomes. And convincing teachers, administrators, and parents that experimental curricula or interventions should be randomly allocated to their classes, schools, or districts will not be an easy task.

Designing a good study that facilitates the evaluation of educational outcomes should not be viewed as a mysterious process. Yet we suspect that part of the problem in educational evaluation has to do with the "culture of evaluation." Many new educational projects are developed with grants from well-meaning nongovernmental organizations or government agencies that typically specify that an evaluator must be involved in the process. Simply hiring a well-respected evaluator or consultant will often satisfy the grantor, but there is often little program accountability beyond that. Frequently the focus is exclusively on descriptive summative evaluations, which may indeed play an important role but permit us to miss the opportunity to evaluate the larger picture.

In general, it's much more difficult to attribute an effect to something that happened a long time ago than to something that happened more recently. This is because a lot of other things that might provoke or explain a change in behavior or attitudes may have occurred in the intervening time. Yet, if we wish to demonstrate effective environmental education programs, we must demonstrate that they lead to long-term changes in student behavior. Often, project evaluations are completed at the end of programs, and few have planned monitoring that occurs over a longer time frame to see how well the education really sticks.

Programs often have multiple goals, only some of which have anything to do with environmental education. For instance, when evaluating the California Outdoor School Program,[6] which combines many different outdoor activities with different objectives into a one-week residence-camp program, which are the activities being evaluated? And, while it may be possible to modify a drug to have different mixes of components, is it going to be as easy to modify a complex environmental education program that, by design, mixes experiences? Or is it valid to evaluate the entire program?

The evaluation of the California Outdoor School Program was designed to incorporate immediate, intermediate, and longer-term time scales in its evaluation. However, it had a strange mix of desired results that included improved student self-esteem, improved student classroom attendance, decreased classroom disciplinary actions, increased high school completion, and increased interest and ability in science classes, but it did not address what we viewed as the key question of an environmental education program: did students demonstrate environmentally responsible behavior?

Testing and evaluation clearly have an important role in educational reform, but do scores on standardized tests allow us to evaluate education, or do they just allow us to evaluate how students do on standardized tests? What if teachers teach to the tests (which is what many feel is happening in response to the No Child Left Behind Act)? What if, in the context of environmental education, evaluators ask the easy questions, simply because they can be easily asked and evaluated? And what are the easy questions? Probably the ones that evaluate attitudes. But it is not only attitudes we seek to change; we also want to change actions. Having a population that loves watching nature shows on television is great, as long as the population acts in ways that preserve and protect the nature that it claims to like. We don't think our current population does this, and we fault, among other things that we have mentioned, a lack of comprehensive, well-designed environmental education in our schools.

It is remarkably difficult to identify the proper questions for evaluating an environmental program. How students react to the information presented probably won't surface until long after the educational program or intervention is experienced. Measuring whether students grow to become environmentally responsible citizens as a result of a specific educational intervention may not even be possible or practical. A long-term longitudinal approach may offer feedback, but may prove to be outside the scope (and budget) of the public educational process—not to mention that the clock of adverse environmental impacts is still ticking. Evaluation questions, and indeed environmental education goals, may have to vary by locality, culture, and economic status, to name just a few variables. And what about the very significant issue of locality: what works in New York City probably won't be the same as what works in Johannesburg or Santiago de Chile or rural Idaho. Understanding experiences and context is an important part of teaching respect for nature. Nevertheless, educators must try, and continue to try, to make programs more effective by utilizing the best tools and ideas available. And it certainly would aid this process if funding entities and administrators adopted an atmosphere of open-mindedness regarding new techniques and experiments, whether conventional or otherwise.

We mentioned qualitative evaluation in our discussion of formative assessment as a means to add another dimension to quantitative methods.[7] An interesting aspect of qualitative evaluation is that it can be used effectively to produce a wealth of data from a relatively small number of cases or individuals. It may also prove a useful and cost-effective alternative to cross-sectional evaluations when group sizes are small because of location-specific programs. Typically, qualitative evaluations are carried out through a combination of open-ended interviews, questionnaires or diaries, and direct observation by an evaluator. In some cases, evaluators may even become program participants. While incorporating evaluation into a program may increase costs, we believe it is essential. Creating and nurturing a new culture of evaluation is critical to improving environmental educational outcomes.

On the surface, qualitative evaluation design may seem to contradict the tenets of independent quantitative evaluation, because it may not maintain objective disassociation from what is being studied. The important thing to remember is that one approach does not negate the other. Indeed, they are complementary and often used successfully in tandem. Qualitative evaluation may reveal unforeseen benefits or problems that controlled quantitative evaluation might miss.

Waldorf schools employ an interesting system whereby a single teacher remains with the same class for eight years, ideally from first through eighth grade. The curriculum is augmented by "specialty teachers," who cover topics like music, art, science, and physical education, but the academic subjects are presented by the primary teacher. A common argument against this kind of approach is that, if primary teachers are required to cover such a broad swath of the curriculum, the quality may suffer. But Waldorf proponents maintain that primary teachers are well trained for the challenge and help "walk a pathway of discovery" with their students, rather than function as instruments of information transfer without context.[8] In theory, each Waldorf class takes on a sort of familial aspect that also helps students develop social skills, problem-solving ability, and a sense of community.

In the Waldorf approach, the teacher plays an important and continuing role in the development of students. As time passes, teachers gain significant insights into the needs, limitations, and capabilities of individual students and can taper teaching methods to accommodate them. This level of personalized involvement might be difficult to achieve in a public school context, but incorporating some aspects of the approach might foster valuable qualitative insights that augment program evaluation efforts.

American public schools generally employ class schedules that start the school day with a homeroom period. Typically, homeroom serves an administrative, rather than academic, function and is usually shorter than regular academic classes. It is where general announcements are made, attendance is monitored, and preparations are made for the coming day at school. There is no special training for homeroom teachers.

But what if schools were to change the function of homerooms to provide a daily meeting and discussion place where students could voice concerns and suggestions and provide ongoing feedback on their educational process? If homeroom class periods were extended to academic-period length, and homeroom teachers stayed with the same class throughout middle school or high school, this could develop a version of the community or familial aspects found in Waldorf schools. Homeroom teachers might be specially trained to counsel student in academics or life skills or both, and familiar with qualitative evaluation techniques. Approached in this way, homerooms could provide a remarkable developmental opportunity for all stakeholders. Homeroom teachers would effectively become the liaison between students, teachers, and administrators. Students might get more out of their school experience, and teachers, schools, and districts might gain insight into their own effectiveness through an ongoing qualitative evaluation of curricula and teaching performance.

This idea for homeroom redesign is similar to what the late climatologist Stephen Schneider called a "creativity tithe."[9] He suggested that creativity is born of discourse, of questioning the status quo, and of searching out fresh answers and formulating new ideas. Schneider thought that when curricula becomes overbearing, in the sense that performance and test scores become the only focus in the classroom, something critical and important is lost from the educational process. He suggested that 10 percent of all classroom time be creative time—time when students can freely discuss what is important to them, and when they are encouraged to question their instructors, as long as they take the initiative to offer creative alternatives or solutions.

If the emphasis in testing procedures in American public schools shifted from the standardized multiple-choice testing to the European method of oral exams conducted by instructors, it would provide yet another opportunity for obtaining qualitative data on program effectiveness. In addition, oral testing develops students' critical thinking abilities and communication skills, as they must understand what is asked and formulate and present their responses in "real time." Oral testing costs more, in money and time, than written testing, but we believe the skills that it develops are well worth the cost.

At the college level, much work is being done by the Nobel laureate Carl Wieman on how to restructure science education to make it more effective.[10] Wieman was puzzled by the fact that his undergraduate students did not consistently understand his physics lectures, which he believed to be clear, concise, and logical. He was further mystified by his graduate students, who, after performing well during many years of science education, had little practical or "expert" ability to conduct research. Being a scientist, he decided to apply the scientific method to the teaching of science and initiated a program of structured research into the process of science education. He found that people learn best when they create their own understanding, becoming deeply involved in the cognitive processes of problem solving. The educator's role then becomes one of "coaching" that process to develop expert thinking. Wieman's educational research also shows that slowing down the presentation of course materials so students' short-term memory does not become overloaded, making clear connections between conceptual course material and its application and meaning in the real world, and engaging students in peer collaboration, all produce far better cognitive development and subject retention than traditional pedagogical methods. To effect change, Wieman believes scientific evaluative tools are needed to measure what students learn, and that universities must undergo a change in institutional culture.

For environmental education to succeed in positively affecting behavior, our educational systems must be creative, responsive, and open to honest and unbiased self-critique. Educators must embrace a new culture of evaluation and measure what works by flexibly combining evaluative tools. And they must abandon or modify the tools, programs, and traditions that do not produce results. Our future depends on it.

CHAPTER TEN

And How We Can Fix It

Fixing the issues we have described in this book is a tall order, by any stretch of the imagination. But imagination is precisely what it will take. And fortunately, when it comes to imagination, humans are particularly adept. As perhaps is now clear, we do not pretend to know all the specific educational steps or changes necessary to create a more active environmental consciousness. We have, however, presented a broad spectrum of ideas to consider, as well as some possible directions to take to address the environmental problems facing our planet and ourselves. These are solvable, we think, through education. We have outlined some potential obstacles to this process, which come from institutional, economic, and political shortsightedness, mis- and disinformation, and the division and deterioration of community throughout the world. What information we have presented is offered as food for thought in the hope that it will help create genuinely new approaches to education that can outrun the pace of the environmental degradation brought about by unbridled industrialization and the flawed concept of ever-expanding growth.

By now, two things should be clear. First, we believe the initial step toward fixing environmental education is to thoroughly unravel the construct of it as an entity unto itself. Rather it must be fully integrated into a twenty-first-century educational package. We think environmental education should develop an informed and thereby active citizenry, but we realize that this will not be accomplished solely by incorporating environmental education curricula into national teaching standards. Instead, the tenets of individual responsibility, development of community, social engagement, and appreciation of nature will have to permeate educational systems at all levels. So, we do not simply propose having more or different environmental education classes; rather, we call for the integration of the concepts described in this book into education as a whole. Along with reading, writing, and arithmetic, schools must teach students about the world we live in, our place in it, and how to sustain and protect the ecosystems that support us all.

Second, when we talk about the failure of environmental education, we mean that environmental education has failed to keep pace with environmental degradation. And while some of the environmental curricula available could use some improvement and expansion, for the most part these curricula have never been implemented on a broad public scale. The real failure of environmental education, then, lies with our political institutions that have succumbed to the influence (and money) of lobbyists, business leaders who evidently cannot see past economic growth to sustainability, and even ourselves, for failing to exercise our collective power to change the world.

While writing this book, we had five distinct aims. First, to illustrate that no one can choose to be an environmentalist. It's not a luxury; it's an essential civic responsibility that falls on each and every living person. Second, we aimed to demonstrate that environmental education must not be marginalized but must become an integral part of a reformed education at all levels. Third, we wanted to show that thoughtful educational evaluation is essential and can lead to efficient changes in teaching and learning, leading, we hope, to better environmental outcomes for us all. Fourth, we wished to reinforce the idea that the ability to fix these things is already within humanity's grasp. And lastly, we wanted to promote the celebration of human diversity and a spirit of flexibility and tolerance.

Humanity is at a dangerous crossroad: our world is changing quickly, and anthropogenic changes are likely to increase human suffering, decrease biodiversity, and threaten our future existence. These are by-products of humanity's race to industrialization and affluence, the resulting global frenzy of consumption, and the need to feed close to seven billion people. Physicist Joe Romm describes humanity's use of resources as an (ecological) Ponzi scheme.[1] By their very nature, Ponzi schemes are unsustainable and doomed to collapse. And collapse is out there somewhere in our near future, perhaps as an ecological tipping point, or as rising oceans, or as national political stability becomes a thing of the past.

In February 2009, Dan saw Al Gore speak at a meeting of the American Association for the Advancement of Science, in Chicago. Gore told the story of how John F. Kennedy said America would put a man on the moon in ten years. In fact, with effort and focus, it actually happened sooner. Gore pointed out that, on the day the first human set foot on the moon, the average age of the mission-control engineers was only twenty-eight. The groundbreaking efforts of these young engineers illustrates how, in the presence of common need, where common will exists and support abounds, all manner of things are attainable.

Speaking to an audience filled with college professors, Gore said he believes that today's college students are the ones who share the opportunity and responsibility of solving the environmental problems created over the past century that are now being fully realized. What Gore did not say is that this charge also extends to those who have not yet reached a university. And the responsibility for developing environmentally aware and active citizens, able to rise to that task, rests directly on public environmental education now and in the future.

Shifting to a postcarbon economy will require decisive effort. The civic responsibilities we must adopt are not necessarily going to be easy. Recycling is easier than buying less, but we must buy less. For some, eating vegetables may be less desirable than eating meat, but we must eat less meat. Paying the true price for energy will be difficult, but it is essential. We must learn to use less energy and make sure that what we do use, we use wisely. The well-being of our children and their children— in fact, the fate of humanity—rests on all of us embracing change and working together to wean ourselves off fossil fuel. Governments can help the process by creating incentives for positive actions and disincentives for negative ones. Educators can help bring about change by making sure that students grasp this cooperative responsibility.

Making these necessary sacrifices may appear altruistic, but they really are not. Each and every one of us wants the best for our families. Each and every one of us wants to avoid the food and water shortages and relocation induced by rising temperatures and sea level. As Jared Diamond wrote in his book *Collapse*, the history of humanity is littered with failed societies.[2] Those that manage their natural resources are the ones that persist, while those that overexploit key resources eventually go extinct.

If governmental incentives for sustainability fail, legislation is the likely next step; in fact, many civic responsibilities are currently legislated. There are laws requiring people to pick up after their dogs, not to assault other people, not to play loud music, to drive on the correct side of the street, and so on. Similarly, laws or taxes may be needed to encourage people to consume less, to recycle more, and to protect undeveloped areas. Our societies must develop the political will to pass these kinds of laws, and education must help accomplish this by teaching about sustainable practices. People may be more willing to accept regulations if they understand the benefits their cooperation will bring about.

Education can also do much to make the links between consumption and its consequences obvious. If schools teach students to understand externalities, a product's price could more easily reflect its true environmental costs, and this might stimulate development of more environmentally friendly alternatives. If school curricula encourage the examination of where products come from, political pressure might eliminate subsidies for environmentally harmful things like oil and gas discovery or industrialized agriculture. These subsidies might then be replaced with aggressive subsidies to develop wind, wave, and solar power or to shift to more sustainable ways of growing food. An additional benefit of teaching product origins is that students would know more about the human costs of manufacture, which might help to spread fair market practices that reduce unfair, unsafe, and exploitive working conditions around the world.

Schools must become places where individuals learn how to value diversity and acquire the skills to lead fruitful and involved lives based on a redefinition of success. If educational institutions taught ecology as the overall system in which we exist, and economy as a subset of that system, instead of the other way around, perhaps the blind rush to affluence perpetrated by rampant industrialization would eventually give way to a more holistic approach to living. One that values quality of community, freedom of expression, and respect for nature as highly as the current system values economic prowess and "progress."

Let's revisit, for a moment, our previous mention of imagination. We have written about how humans have overused the planet's natural resources, how unrestrained industrial growth has led to the brink of environmental catastrophe, and how business and political leaders are subject to corruption and the influences of special interest groups. Despite this, we remain cautiously optimistic, and these assaults have not undermined our faith in the human ability to educate our way out of this mess. For every anthropogenic environmental mistake made, there are volumes of enduring literature; for every toxic landfill, there are scores of immensely beneficial technological advances. In the modern world we are fortunate to live in, people are living longer, infant mortality rates are declining, and there is more free time to use as one pleases. And this barely scratches the surface of the human capacity to imagine new realities, to find individual expression in art or science or poetry, and to use these unique traits to better the lives of others and enhance the collective future. We are confident this unique imagination that each and every one of us possesses is the key to learning our sustainable place in the fabric of nature. It is simply a question of will.

Remember the women from the Kenyan Green Belt Movement who started planting trees, and then, suitably empowered, successfully lobbied for human rights? Their movement involved people at a very local scale, which then grew to international proportions. This is a brilliant illustration of a grassroots rise to collective action and power. The civil rights movement in the United States and the fall of apartheid in South Africa are further examples of how people can change long-standing, seemingly unchangeable institutions and policies in a relatively short time when the collective will becomes strong enough. Decent, breathable air and clean, drinkable water are a fundamental right, regardless of political or religious beliefs, regardless of economic or social standing, even regardless of species. Global educational institutions must help us learn these things, but, because they are not moving quickly enough toward that end, the impetus must come from the grassroots. Teachers must take the lead in this effort, wherever possible and however possible.

Increasingly, we have begun to notice that concepts like sustainability and reducing energy usage are popping up in isolated public school classes, despite the fact that these concepts are not part of any formal standardized curriculum. We have heard children in the supermarket telling their parents why one product is better for the environment than another. This is happening because motivated individual teachers are taking it upon themselves to make it happen. They are creating what we hope will be the tip of an iceberg of transformation in public education. A metamorphosis that will elicit global and local action to bring about real and measurable impacts. Education must build on these grassroots successes, and while they may be small or local, they are many. The cornerstones are already in place. The obstacles to success are substantial, but those in the educational trenches must always remember that tipping points work both ways, and there is a point out there somewhere where concepts like sustainability and responsible stewardship acquire their own momentum. This is what some marketing people like to call "viral growth," and such growth can be greatly influenced by the actions of individuals.

One way for teachers to effect grassroots change is to teach students how to vote with their dollars—by making environmentally sensible purchases. Such action can have an immediate effect. Resources like the Web site Goodguide.com provide information on a number of aspects associated with various products, including health issues, environmental impacts, and the company's level of social responsibility. Suitably educated, consumers can make choices that will lead to decreased emissions, pollution, and use of dangerous chemicals.

An essential thing for students to understand is that what they buy determines what will be produced. If people decide to buy organic, producers will grow organic. More demand for organically and locally grown food creates trends that serve to reduce prices, provide local market incentives for new investment, provide new local career options, and decrease demand for industrially farmed foods, all at the same time. The more teachers do to help students understand the environmental costs and benefits of products they and their families purchase, the more likely local environmental benefits will be realized and sustainable thinking will spread.

Curricula must evolve to reflect the importance of not only what we teach but also how we teach it, as these things are closely intertwined. Environmental awareness does not necessarily lead to responsible environmental action, but it is precisely expedient action that is necessary if humanity's environmental problems are to be successfully addressed. If, as Al Gore says, the responsibility for fixing humankind's environmental messes rests with today's students, then educators must work quickly to enhance students' capacity for the kind of critical and creative thinking that leads to action. This cannot be accomplished through the presentation of theoretical information alone. Taking a look at the California science content standards, we see that, on the surface, they seem to focus on ecology and biodiversity. But the recurrent emphasis is on understanding the scientific process, which is good but incomplete.[3] We think that, by adding a reasonable, age-appropriate focus on environmental problems, along with a significant social component, students should be able to put two and two together and change their behavior in ecologically responsible ways. What environmental education must accomplish is to become relevant to the lives of the students who are expected to do something with the information. What kinds of things, then, must happen to facilitate this?

Ideally, our educational institutions need physical makeovers. Spending every day in schools that architecturally isolate students from nature by their very design is a powerful object lesson, regardless of what is being taught inside the walls. It is hard for students to make relevant connections to natural processes when they sit inside air-conditioned rooms that open on asphalt playgrounds or groomed lawns with concrete walkways. Learning spaces that incorporate elements like cross-ventilation, geothermal heating and cooling, solar electricity, indigenous plant species and wooded areas, waste reclamation systems, vegetable gardens, and outdoor classroom areas are not only teaching entities but are working, relevant representations of our relationship to our natural surroundings. Approval of any such redesign, however, must run the gauntlet of an institutional approval process and may therefore have little practical significance to this discussion, given prevailing bureaucracies and fiscal constraints. We have made a few suggestions as to how this problem might be addressed (see the appendix), but it may be more practical to focus on working within existing systems for short-term effects while continuing to push hard for the long-term changes.

Clearly, education does not currently go far enough to teach students about the wonders of the earth and the diversity of life. As Senegalese scholar Baba Dioum has said, "In the end we will conserve only what we love. We will love only what we understand. We will understand only what we are taught."[4] Exploring nature on one's own terms, both in school and with friends and family, helps to instill a sense of wonder and respect for nature and, to achieve this, schools must somehow get students outside.

Throughout the entirety of K–12 education, we believe, significant time must be devoted to the exploration of natural places. These natural encounters ought not be approached as isolated field trips; rather, they should be fully integrated into standard curricula. This can involve introducing students to different natural habitats; but to some extent, where students go is of less importance than making sure they are guided by educators who are comfortable working outside and using nature as a teacher. We remember the first time we were encouraged to look down at a patch of ground and saw the variety of insects that lived there. Concentrating on their movements and interactions revealed greater details of their world, a world quite different from ours but, at the same time, a part of it. Through experiences like these, we began to understand something about the diversity of life, habitats, and interdependence of species. Learning to simply open one's eyes and "see" the world is an important step toward learning to understand and respect the complex systems that support biodiversity. Without such natural encounters, it is hard to imagine how any love of nature might develop, and without love, there is little reason for protection or any sense of stewardship.

Each passing postindustrial generation loses another bit of natural connection and awareness as cities continue to grow, wilderness areas decline, and what little wild space remains becomes less and less wild. In urban centers, open fields and empty lots are fast becoming only the memories of older generations who ran and played there as children. Young people growing up in cities have little knowledge of these places, and what they experience of wild places is often only what they view from the decks of cruise ships or the windows of automobiles. Kids gather in shopping malls instead of parks. Children identify cars, rather than birds. In an effort to keep children safe from danger, likely exaggerated by the media, our societies turn to controlled and supervised play dates, and unsupervised outdoor play becomes a thing of the past. Parents provide cellular phones and drive their children everywhere, including to and from school. This may seem safer than the alternative, but a side effect is that children no longer learn how to be alone and self-reliant, and so tend to grow up believing that all things unknown are to be avoided. Windows no longer open, air-conditioning is the norm, food comes from the market . . . it is no wonder the environment suffers. Advertising pulls society toward consumption and acquisition, leaving little room for natural and less-consumptive pursuits. In college field biology classes, which only decades ago were the meeting places for those with a fierce curiosity about the outdoors, it is becoming increasingly difficult to find students who actually want to spend time in the field. Instead, many prefer to stay inside and do lab work where cellular coverage is abundant and insects are few. These trends do not bode well for the environmental health of our species and our planet.

Education alone cannot reverse these trends; it will take family and community involvement as well. What schools can do, however, is attempt to raise parental and community awareness of these problems and provide alternatives wherever possible. Shouldn't some change in behavior begin in kindergartens, where students living near their community schools can walk to them? Schools might encourage concerned parents to walk their children to school or, better yet, organize enhanced neighborhood supervision provided by parents and volunteers, so that children can safely walk or bike to and from school on their own. These are perhaps small steps, but they are easily realized at little or no expense to school districts and may provide a turning point in the collective rush away from the outdoors.

Getting students outside in urban environments presents real challenges to schools, both logistically and economically. But it is not in society's long-term best interests to cut outdoor education experiences simply because they are difficult to accomplish. Ways must be found to overcome the roadblocks. Initially, it may be necessary to allocate money for urban outdoor education programs based on physical proximity to natural areas. In other words, the farther away from natural areas a school is, the more money it would receive to ensure that students experience natural encounters. If funding is tight, enrollment of students in camplike outdoor education programs affiliated with public schools might be biased so that students from urban schools attend more frequently than students from schools in more natural surroundings. Ideally, we hope our societies will grow to understand the importance of outdoor education (and education in general) to the quality of our communities and assure that funding for education is adequate and not marginalized in favor of supporting special interests.

In chapter 6 we wrote about how growing food in school gardens has proven an effective teaching tool for a variety of disciplines at almost all developmental levels. Whether the gardens lead to the incorporation of student-produced fresh foods into school lunch programs, or they become the basis for community involvement through greening and beautification of urban areas, they provide students with a practical connection to nature. School gardens provide teachers with outdoor platforms for teaching math and science classes without leaving the school campus. All schools, at all levels, should have gardens, and all students should experience working in them as a part of a standard curriculum.

Public education must focus on teaching ecology. An understanding of ecological processes is essential if people are to understand how humanity is affecting life on earth. As we mentioned in chapter 3, students should learn about nonlinear relationships and tipping points. They should learn about synergistic effects, where the whole is greater than the sum of its parts. Importantly, learning these concepts will help involved citizens ask critical questions and evaluate scientific information to gain a clearer idea of the state of the environment.

Curricula must vary according to where a school is situated. Although educational standards must be met, exactly how that is accomplished is a decision for each district, perhaps even each teacher, to make. In urban settings, more effort may need to go into simply providing opportunities for students to experience the natural world, while in rural communities, where students may take nature for granted, more effort may be necessary to help them see things in a more global way. Well-trained environmental educators play a vital role here by providing the activities and context for promoting effective environmental awareness.

Science can easily be taught outdoors, because nature provides endless examples of scientific function and processes that can be tied to standardized curricula. The study of art and literature also benefits from classes conducted outside if curricula are tied to natural observations. Teaching outdoors and encouraging students to think about how writers, painters, or poets might have experienced and expressed nature may help students develop personal insights or an increased appreciation for the natural world, beyond what they would have obtained from the same material studied inside a classroom.

Creating learning projects, both in and outside the classroom, that cross the lines of traditional topical boundaries will serve to integrate, not isolate, relevant ecology and environmental science lessons. These will stimulate critical thinking abilities and help students become better able to assimilate and apply knowledge from different disciplines. Such projects must be age-appropriate and might, as a starting point, use the guidelines proposed by the North American Association for Environmental Education (NAAEE),[5] which nicely combine knowledge of biological systems, physical sciences, and social and political science into an integrated set of objectives. The guidelines are also designed to provide the tools educated citizens need in order to become more active participants in a democracy. Teaching tools such as oil vulnerability exercises can provide a compelling and relevant way to integrate environmental education into math studies.[6] In these exercises, students analyze household products (many derived from petroleum) and foods (many of which use petroleum-based fertilizers and require transportation) to determine what percentage of product costs are based on petroleum products. Simulations might then be made of the future world, where less petroleum is available at greater expense, and costs and benefits of creating resilient alternatives to fossil fuels can be practically visualized.

A flexible and open-minded approach to curricula is an important component of redesigning education, but we strongly believe that even the best possible curricula will not translate into action unless it includes a strong and relevant social component. Students must experience active involvement in a community where theoretical knowledge is practically applied and actions and reactions have personal significance and value to the individual and community alike. This is perhaps one of the most challenging aspects of environmental education, and there are no easy road maps to success. It will likely be an ongoing experiment that will draw on all the creativity and skill that educators can muster. Teaching basic civics alone won't do it. Students need to know their voices matter in the political process, and the best place to begin that process, we believe, is their communities. Civics programs must expand to focus not only on providing a historical perspective of political systems but also on providing students with knowledge needed to transform their communities into places that reflect how they would like to live. Civics must help students become active citizens, with all the associated rights and responsibilities.

Schools must teach how legislation is practically crafted, how representatives are influenced, and how organized citizen groups can affect legislative process. Civics courses might even go so far as to engage students in community projects that include getting involved in the process of legislative action, such as the appropriation or development of municipal land for recreational use, or the banning of nonbiodegradable materials in school food packaging. Students might focus on raising awareness about a particular issue and employ their art, communication, and science skills to bring that issue to their community. As in the Food From the Hood program we described in chapter 6, students can create community gardens on public or private land, then teach and encourage local residents to grow their own food for consumption and profit. Such projects might entail lobbying city or school councils and politicians for necessary approvals, or contacting and using media and community outreach when public pressure is needed to prevent the political process from stalling their efforts. It is through this kind of active engagement that students will learn how to become involved, effective citizens of the communities, states, and countries in which they live.

Such active, integrative experiences can teach the power of collaborating to reach a common goal as groups identify and utilize the individual strengths and knowledge of their members. Each student can contribute in some meaningful way. The most articulate might be those who speak at meetings or presentations. Those with art and technical skills can produce graphics or Web sites to support the collective effort. Everyone can help with research. The point of the exercise is to have students experience the process of making measurable impacts. This is fundamental to an involved citizenry, and an involved citizenry is fundamental to improving our environment.

Where there is no political or administrative support for incorporation of these integrative projects in regular curricula, they might instead be implemented as extracurricular activities that cater to a subset of students, much like soccer and football. Most students who play K–12 sports will not go on to become professional soccer or football players. But, by participating in sports, they develop lifelong interpersonal and athletic skills. Similarly, students who get involved early in life in political action may not go on to become politicians, but they will understand that change is possible through individual and community action, and will likely grow to be involved and politically active adults. This involvement, coupled with integrated environmental education that teaches critical thinking, is where the best hope lies for changing our environmental future for the better.

It is critically important to know what works and what doesn't if our schools are to produce expedient changes in student attitudes and behavior. Good programs must get better, and bad ones must be dropped or modified. For this to happen, the educational system must change the present culture of evaluation. In chapter 9, we wrote that evaluation is something many disciplines struggle with, and proper implementation is challenging and complicated. But scientifically based evaluation can help us optimize our efforts. At its essence, performing proper evaluation is like conducting a scientific experiment. Some methods of evaluation, like the evaluation tool developed by the North American Association for Environmental Education, focus on evaluating programmatic content, but not the effect such content has on students' abilities or behavior. This kind of evaluation is only one step toward more comprehensive process that must determine effective ways to teach complex ideas, as well as whether students modify their behavior as a result of a specific curriculum or teaching method. We believe the best way to ensure cost-efficient and effective education is through high-quality project evaluation that draws on diverse evaluative methodologies and looks at both long- and short-term impacts.

This new culture of evaluation must include longitudinal studies of behavioral changes that reduce consumption, energy usage, and the production of greenhouse gasses. An example of this might include offering an environmental education class covering sustainable practices and externalities to a randomly selected group of students. In a home economics class the following semester, this same group would then be monitored and compared to a control group of students who did not take the environmental class. Asking students from both groups what products they purchase, and why, might provide insight into whether purchasing decisions, made within the context of the home economics class, changed—in the group that took the environmental class—to favor more environmentally friendly products. If this kind of sensible evaluation is used "adaptively," programmatic content should change over time to become increasingly effective. This will require coordination between evaluators, educators, and administrators. We acknowledge that evaluation, as we envision it, is time-consuming and expensive, but it is another essential tool for acting quickly and effectively to save our planet from widespread environmental collapse. As political administrations come and go, political agendas change, so one aspect of evaluation worthy of discussion is: what is the best way to assure this new culture of evaluation remains independent and able to resist politicization? One possible solution may come from the American Constitution, which set up government with a system of checks and balances. Decisions are made by consensus of the independent arms of government. Management of educational evaluation could be approached in this way by creating independent administrative branches (quantitative, qualitative, and psychological, for example). To enact policy or programmatic change, these branches would have to reach a consensus. This might help educators resist whatever the current political agenda may be and instead favor effective, applied evaluation methods in an objective manner. Good evaluation cannot happen without open-minded administrators committed to efficient methods of measuring impacts.

The No Child Left Behind Act and the subsequent Race to the Top competition attempt to quantify school and teacher performance, which on the surface seems like a great idea. But after talking with teachers, one often comes away with a less-than-positive opinion of the mechanics and effectiveness of the program. Evaluation of teacher effectiveness is not such a clear-cut task, and student performance on standardized tests leaves much to be desired as the measure of a good teacher.

Teachers need ongoing evaluation, but not solely in the form of standardized tests handed down from administrators or politicians who may have no direct contact with teachers or students. We think teacher effectiveness is best judged by a combination of sources that includes quality administrators with excellent management and motivational skills, opinions of students and colleagues, and artfully designed and culturally relevant before-after, control-impact surveys. If educational institutions are going to be successful in cultivating active and aware citizens, nothing less than effective, motivated teachers and administrators will do.

What about ineffective teachers or poor administrators who are unable to properly manage the kinds of integrative projects that, we propose, are necessary for change? What about those who remain in the school ranks because of tenure rather than merit? What about those who do not pass the evaluation process? Here again, the onus is on creative and open-minded administrators who can identify underperforming teachers with potential for improvement, and then help them to become excellent by providing them additional training, mentorship programs, and all available resources the district has to offer. Those teachers who lack motivation or are unable to improve their skills should be moved to nonteaching jobs within the district, if such opportunities can be found or created, or their employment should be terminated and contracts bought out where necessary. This brings up the controversial topics of tenure and unions.

Academic tenure (the right not to have employment terminated without just cause) was originally conceived to protect educators from capricious termination. But the reasons for its establishment may no longer be relevant in K–12 education, and the way it is earned and sustained may represent two big reasons that many public schools are faltering. Typically, tenure is granted almost automatically after one or two years of teaching. During the first years, teachers are still learning about their schools and developing their lectures. Long before they can be properly evaluated, they are tenured. Teachers need special credentials or degrees to be hired, but these credentials are no indication of teaching ability. There is typically little posthiring teacher evaluation, and compensation is generally based on the amount of time spent on the job, rather than on merit. These are not practices that promote excellence, and they must be changed. Unions typically support the existing system, but it is time they, along with all factions of the status quo, did some critical self-evaluation. Teachers' rights must be protected, but not at the expense of quality education. If these two things are in conflict, it is a good indication of systemic failure. Every faction of every educational institution should point clearly toward bettering the lives of the students it seeks to educate.

The District of Columbia's former superintendent of education, Michelle Rhee, proposed addressing this problem by offering a controversial option to tenured teachers, whereby they could earn up to $130,000 per year but had to agree to give up their tenure and submit to a yearlong teacher effectiveness evaluation.[7] New teachers who selected this option would have started at modest salaries with the potential for quickly gaining substantial raises based on performance. Teachers who did not select this option and retained tenure would have had a lower overall pay scale with lower fixed raises. There was union resistance to Ms. Rhee's approach, and it is unclear whether this or other strategies would be successful. However, ideas like this one are likely a necessary part of effective educational reform. Moving away from a system that instills tenure automatically, and toward one that promotes and rewards individual merit, has little risk.

In early 2010, California's legislature approved measures aimed at improving schools by allowing parents to transfer their children out of the one thousand lowest-performing schools in the state to better ones, even to schools out of the child's district.[8] The measures will provide parents with greater influence in the process of fixing poorly performing schools: they can petition for changes in teaching and administrative staff, for conversion of public schools to charter schools, or for closure. The California teachers' union opposes these measures because they believe it may lead to overloading recipient schools as parents transfer their children out of poorly performing ones. The union also worries that these measures will effectively leave poorly performing schools without needed reforms and, in the end, students will suffer. However, while this legislation is new and unproven, it offers another opportunity to evaluate whether these kinds of reforms will work. School reform is necessary, but it must be sweeping, ongoing, and creative. We believe that new approaches being tried across the globe, conventional or unconventional, are worth watching and evaluating and potentially adopting. There is likely no single solution, as humans are a diverse bunch, but without experimentation and creativity there will be little progress.

Making educational institutions better is tough and complicated work. There are no uniform solutions, because what works in one classroom will probably be different from what works in another. But high-quality, motivated teachers are a critical constant, and society must value and support them, as well as listen to what they have to say about the directions schools should take to become more effective. As discussed in chapter 5, teacher compensation, while it must be competitive, may not be the sole motivator. Perhaps things like increasing teacher support by supplying teachers with more assistants or interns—and offering teachers flexibility in choosing and presenting curricula, paid educational benefits, teacher enrichment opportunities, support for outdoor education, and open-door administration policies—might play an important part in finding and keeping the excellent, motivated teachers society needs in order to effect change.

Education is critical to the future well-being of all nations, and integrated environmental education is critical to the future well-being of our planet's ecology. Current public educational institutions tend to emphasize disciplines that provide economic value to nations, over those that simply enrich lives or develop community involvement. National and state education standards reflect this bias. The challenges that face coming generations will be substantial as the earth's population swells and resources dwindle. Bolstering national economies will not fix these problems. Blindly following a model of infinite economic growth, when we all dwell on a planet with a finite capacity to support life, is obviously reckless. If humanity is to preserve its place on earth, we need creativity, flexibility, compassion, and understanding, along with technological and scientific acumen, all of which must be introduced, developed, and reinforced by our educational institutions.

Many of these changes and reforms are expensive to implement, and finding the money to pay for them is never easy, especially in times of economic uncertainty and hardship. Citizens will probably have to pay higher taxes, and this is always a major point of public contention. Simply throwing public money at educational institutions that don't work well is a bad idea, so ways must be found to hold those institutions accountable to the public. Programs put in place by the No Child Left Behind Act attempt this, but their methodologies are flawed and they do little to develop the capability for critical thought that is necessary for good citizenship. Transparency and real accountability must be part of any reform effort if we hope to overcome popular resistance to paying more for education. Recent financial bailouts made by governments around the world illustrate that public education takes a backseat to economic development when it comes to national funding priorities. We appropriate monies to shore up failing industries but do relatively little to assure the intellectual development of our peoples. This must change, and soon.

Adequate funding for schools is not a liberal or a conservative issue. It is in society's best interests to have an educated populace. Allowing politically motivated divisions in our societies to deadlock the prioritization of education is misplaced and unconstructive. If parents and students can come to view critical thinking and community awareness as survival tools for the future, then perhaps adequate pressure will be brought to bear on political and business leaders to enlarge the focus of education in order to develop these things.

How can we fix environmental education? Can it be fixed at all? We acknowledge that part of what we propose in this book may seem, to some readers, a somewhat utopian paradigm shift. But such a shift is necessary to preserve our future, not for "tree-hugging environmentalist" reasons, but rather to avoid the ominous alternatives that may result from following humanity's present course. Because humans are variable, education must be variable. Because societies are variable and they change, education must be flexible and adaptive. There are no absolute solutions or perfect methods, and what seems promising today will likely grow tired over time. But we are great believers in the human spirit and in the unique capacity we all possess to decide to change outcomes. While still imperfect, adequate technologies for change exist today, and the tools and skills for fixing our predicament are well within reach. We need only the will, coupled with common sense and education, to choose a better and sustainable world for ourselves and for the generations to come.

GREENING SCHOOLS FOR ALTERNATIVE EDUCATION

We live and work in the second largest public school district in the United States. Los Angeles Unified School District sports a total enrollment of more than 680,000 students per year and has more than one thousand schools, including magnet centers. Large urban public school districts like this one are typically strapped for funds, especially in light of several years' worth of global economic hardship. Implementing many of the ideas we've discussed in this book takes money, and lots of it. But those expenditures are not so huge as to present major obstacles to changing the face of our public schools. Consider the following "what if" scenario that, if implemented in urban public school districts, might accomplish much at a relatively minimal cost.

What if public school districts in large urban communities were to hire a team of six or so professionals whose job would be to travel from high school to high school as recruiters and advisors for the "greening up our schools" idea we mention in chapter 4? The team might consist of an architect or general contractor, a risks assessment person, a sustainability specialist, a landscape contractor, a marketing specialist, and a project coordinator. For clarity, let's call this team the Green Advisory Team (GAT). Let's start these folks at a good teacher's salary of $70,000 per year, plus benefits, which sums up to $466,200 per year for the group. Let's round this up to $500,000 to include the team's expenses for traveling around their district.

The GAT's initial task would be to recruit groups of interested students in each school who agree to take on the responsibility of conceptualizing and developing projects to transform their school campus into something greener and more sustainable, and, most important, into a place that reflects the style and tastes of the student body. For this idea to work, it will be necessary to stop thinking of school campuses as static places and to instead regard them as learning centers in continual transition.

The second step in the process would be for the student group to poll the student body (through in-class presentations followed by public-comment meetings) and develop a consensus action plan. This would be carried out under the guidance, *not the instruction*, of the GAT, which means students would take the primary initiative to determine the best approach for gaining results, researching ideas, determining feasibility, creating presentations, conducting meetings, and tallying results. In this phase of the process, the GAT would point students to places where they might obtain the skills or information necessary to realize a given project, but the full responsibility for any project would always rest with the student group.

Money for any action plan that has been approved by the student body, and which has won GAT approval for safety, insurance, and feasibility, would not come from the school district.

Students would have to make use of the available "social capital" present in their respective communities (we use the term *social capital* here to mean the resources, person power, in-kind donations of services and materials, and funding needed for the realization of a project). The resources available in each community would tend to dictate the magnitude of the projects, and the GAT would assist the student group in the planning stages to gather accurate information on available levels of social capital. Supplemental funding for projects might also be obtained through government agencies and community nonprofits interested in sustainability, school revitalization, or educational reform. In some cases, money might be earned as a direct result of student projects that offer products or services to the public for profit.

Students involved in such a program would need time and special academic guidance. To be practical, the student commitment would probably need to be at least several semesters in duration, if not longer. One way to facilitate this might be to remove participating students from regular class schedules (with parental support, of course) and assign a single full-time teacher or counselor per school whose job would be to help students deal with any academic challenges encountered in the project development and realization process. Ideally, students would be graded only on the success of their projects, but if that is too radical an idea for public education, the assigned teacher would have to make sure the student group was able to pass tests mandated by the district. The school district would have the additional cost of one senior teacher per school, so let's add another $70,000 (plus benefits) for each high school we think the GAT could handle in any given year. Let's be ambitious and choose thirty senior high schools per district per year (in Los Angeles, thirty high schools represents about one-quarter of the district total). This would add another $2,408,700 or so, bringing the program's total cost to just under $3 million dollars per year. This seems like a lot of money until you compare it to the typical annual budget of any large urban center, which can easily run into the billions.

Some might consider this another example of utopian thinking. We think the level of social engagement this project would foster, coupled with the variety of practical, entrepreneurial, and communication skills that students would undoubtedly come away with, would prove a remarkable means of shaping active citizens—citizens who would go on to flourish in their communities, in public service, or in higher education. The key aspect of such programs would be their commitment to sustainability. The primary goal of any project would be to increase school energy efficiency or reduce consumption, create green areas on campus, or promote sustainable practices in the community.

If such a program were undertaken and it proved to be successful, it could be expanded to include a larger percentage of high schools within a district at a lower cost per school, as the central administrative structure would already be in place. We believe this is well worth pursuing.

NOTES

ONE. THE PROBLEM(S)

1. R. K. Pachauri and A. Reisinger, eds., *Climate Change 2007 Synthesis Report*, Intergovernmental Panel on Climate Change Fourth Assessment Report (Geneva: IPCC, 2007), 30, 39.

2. N. H. Stern, *The Economics of Climate Change: The Stern Review* (Cambridge: Cambridge University Press, 2007), 640.

3. J. Jowit and P. Wintour, "Cost of Tackling Climate Change Has Doubled, Warns Stern," *The Guardian,* June 26, 2008, 2.

4. M. Kennedy, D. Mrofka, and C. von der Borch, "Snowball Earth Termination by Destabilization of Equatorial Permafrost Methane Clathrate," *Nature* 453 (2008): 642–645.

5. "Large Methane Release Could Cause Abrupt Climate Change as Happened 635 Million Years Ago," report originating at the University of California, Riverside, *ScienceDaily,* May 2008, www.sciencedaily.com/releases/2008/05/080528140255.htm. F. Pearce, "Arctic Meltdown Is a Threat to Humanity," *New Scientist* (March 28–April 3, 2009): 32–36.

6. M. Vellinga and R. A. Wood, "Impacts of Thermohaline Circulation Shutdown in the Twenty-first Century," *Climatic Change* 91 (2008): 43–63.

7. J.C. Orr, V.J. Fabry, O. Aumont, L. Bopp, S.C. Doney et al., "Anthropogenic Ocean Acidification over the Twenty-first Century and Its Impact on Calcifying Organisms," *Nature* 437 (2005): 681–686.

8. B. Worm, E.B. Barbier, N. Beaumont, J.E. Duff, and C. Folke et al., "Impacts of Biodiversity Loss on Ocean Ecosystem Services," *Science* 314 (2006): 787–790.

9. Food and Agricultural Organization of the United Nations, *The State of World Fisheries and Aquaculture: 2008,* State of World Fisheries and Aquaculture series (Rome: FAO, 2009), 66.

10. T. Malthus, *An Essay on the Principle of Population,* ed. J. Johnson (London, 1798; reprint, New York: Oxford University Press, 2008), 13.

11. P. Glover, "Aramco Chief Debunks Peak Oil," *Energy Tribune,* 2008, www.energytribune.com/articles.cfm?aid=764); M.C. Lynch, "The New Pessimism about Petroleum Resources: Debunking the Hubbert Model (and Hubbert Modelers)," *Minerals and Energy—Raw Materials Report* 18, no. 1 (2003): 21–32.

12. M.R. Simmons, *Twilight in the Desert* (Hoboken, NJ: John Wiley & Sons, 2005).

13. C. Robertson and C. Krauss, "Gulf Spill Is the Largest of Its Kind, Scientists Say," *New York Times,* August 2, 2010.

14. C. Robertson and E. Rosenthal, "Agency Orders Use of a Less Toxic Chemical in Gulf," *New York Times,* May 20, 2010.

15. R. Hopkins, *The Transition Handbook: From Oil Dependency to Local Resilience* (White River Junction, VT: Chelsea Green, 2008), 24.

16. R.L. Hirsch, R.H. Bezdek, and R.M. Wendling, *Peaking of World Oil Production: Impacts, Mitigation and Risk Management* (Washington, DC: U.S. Department of Energy, National Energy Technology Laboratory, 2005).

17. J.H. Kunstler, *The Long Emergency: Surviving the Converging Catastrophes of the Twenty-First Century* (New York: Grove Press, 2006).

18. Senate Foreign Relations Committee, Statement of Vice Admiral Dennis McGinn, USN, retired, member of the Military Advisory Board, hearing before the Senate Foreign Relations Committee, *Climate Change and Global Security: Challenges, Threats and Global Opportunities,*

2009, http://epw.senate.gov/public/index/cfm?FuseAction=FilesVie w&FileStore_id=fa102432-4ea9-4228-b6a5-7c6860623548c.

19. CNA Military Advisory Board, *National Security and the Threat of Climate Change* (Alexandria, VA: CNA Corporation, 2007), http:// securityandclimate.cna.org/report/National%20Security%20and%20 the%20Threat%20of%20Climate%20Change.pdf. CNA Military Advisory Board, *Powering America's Defense: Energy and the Risks to National Security* (Alexandria, VA: CNA Corporation, 2009), www.cna .org/documents/PoweringAmericasDefense.pdf.

20. J.B.C. Jackson, "Ecological Extinction and Evolution in the Brave New Ocean," *PNAS* 105, no. 1 (2008): 11458–11465.

21. C. Moore, S. Moore, M. Leecaster, and S.B. Weisberg, "A Comparison of Plastic and Plankton in the North Pacific Central Gyre," *Marine Pollution Bulletin* 42, no. 12 (2001): 1297–1300.

22. H.E. Daly, "Climate Policy: From 'Know How' to 'Do Now,'" keynote address to the American Meteorological Society, workshop on federal climate policy, November 2007, www.climatepolicy.org/ ?p=65.

TWO. FOUNDATIONS

1. K.C. Armitage, *The Nature Study Movement: The Forgotten Popularizer of America's Conservation Ethic* (Lawrence: University Press of Kansas, 2009).

2. H.D. Thoreau, *Walden; or, Life in the Woods* (Boston: Ticnor and Fields, 1854). J. Muir, *John Muir: Nature Writings* (New York: Library of America, 1997).

3. L. Lear, *Rachel Carson: Witness for Nature* (New York: Holt Paperbacks, 1998), 451.

4. Organization for Economic Co-operation and Development, *Green at Fifteen?* (Paris: Programme for International Student Assessment, 2006).

5. California State Board of Education, *Science Content Standards for California Public Schools: Kindergarten Through Grade Twelve* (Sacramento: California State Board of Education, 1998).

6. *No Child Left Inside Act of 2008*, H.R. 3036, Govtrack.us, www.govtrack.us/congress/bill.xpd?bill=h110–3036.

7. *Education and the Environment Initiative*, CA Assembly Bill 1548, 2003; *Education and the Environment Initiative*, CA Assembly Bill 1721, 2005.

8. T. Jefferson, *A Bill for the More General Diffusion of Knowledge*, 1778. This bill was presented to the House of Delegates in 1778 and 1780, but was not passed. See http://candst.tripod.com/jefflaw1.htm.

9. J. Dewey, *The Essential Dewey*, ed. L. Hickman and T. Alexander, vol. 1: *Pragmatism, Education, Democracy* (Bloomington: Indiana University Press, 1998), 231.

10. T. Snyder, ed., *120 Years of American Education: A Statistical Portrait* (Washington, DC: National Center for Educational Statistics, 1993). Statistics available from the *National Assessment of Adult Literacy*, National Center for Education Statistics, http://nces.ed.gov/naal/lit_history.asp.

11. N. Postman, *Amusing Ourselves to Death: Public Discourse in the Age of Show Business* (New York, Penguin, 2006), xix.

12. M.R. Kerbel, *If It Bleeds, It Leads: An Anatomy of Television News* (Boulder, CO: Westview Press, 2001).

THREE. WHAT WENT WRONG

1. J. Carter, transcript of the "crisis of confidence" speech, July 15, 1979, http://millercenter.org/scripps/archive/speeches/detail/3402.

2. R.W. Reagan, transcript of a speech to the Republican National Convention, July 17, 1980, http://millercenter.org/scripps/archive/speeches/detail/3406.

3. National Association of Homebuilders Public Affairs and Economics, "Housing Facts, Figures and Trends," NAHB Public Affairs and NAHB Economics, March 2006, www.soflo.org/report/NAHBhousingfactsMarch2006.pdf.

4. U.S. Census Bureau, *Families and Living Arrangements*, "Current Population Survey (CPS) Reports," table HH-4: "Households by Size: 1960 to Present," 2009, www.census.gov/population/www/socdemo/hh-fam.html.

5. U.S. Social Security Administration, Social Security Online: History, "Research Note #25: Ponzi Schemes versus Social Security," 2009, http://www.ssa.gov/history/ponzi.htm.

6. North Carolina State University, "Mayday 23: World Population Becomes More Urban Than Rural," *ScienceDaily,* May 25, 2007, www.sciencedaily.com/releases/2007/05/070525000642.htm.

7. D. Sobel, *Beyond Ecophobia: Reclaiming the Heart in Nature Education,* Orion Society Nature Literacy Series, vol. 1 (Great Barrington, MA: Orion Society, 1996).

8. R. L. Carson, *Silent Spring* (Boston: Houghton-Mifflin, 1962).

9. Ducks Unlimited, "DU's Carbon Sequestration Program," n.d., www.ducks.org/Conservation/EcoAssets/1306/CarbonSequestration.html.

10. J. A. Lichatowich, *Salmon Without Rivers: A History of the Pacific Salmon Crisis* (Washington DC: Island Press, 1999).

FOUR. ACCOUNTABILITY AND INSTITUTIONAL
MIND-SET

1. D. W. Orr, *Down to the Wire: Confronting Climate Collapse* (New York: Oxford University Press, 2009).

2. *American Clean Energy and Security Act of 2009,* HR 2454, 111th Cong., 1st sess., http://frwebgate.access.gpo.gov/cgi-bin/getdoc.cgi?dbname=111_cong_bills&docid=f:h2454pcs.txt.pdf. *Clean Energy Jobs and American Power Act,* S 1733, 111th Cong.,1st sess., http://frwebgate.access.gpo.gov/cgi-bin/getdoc.cgi?dbname=111_cong_bills&docid=f:s1733is.txt.pdf.

3. S. Gupta, D. A. Tirpak, N. Burger, J. Gupta, N. Hohne et al., "Policies, Instruments and Co-operative Arrangements, in *Climate Change 2007: Mitigation, Contribution of Working Group III to the Fourth Assessment Report of the Intergovernmental Panel on Climate Change,* ed. B. Metz, O.R. Davidson, P.R. Bosch, R. Dave, and L.A. Meyer (Cambridge: Cambridge University Press, 2007), 775.

4. U.S. Environmental Protection Agency, *History of the Clean Air Act,* 2008, www.epa.gov/air/caa/caa_history.html.

5. Commission of the European Communities, *Communication from the Commission to the European Parliament, the Council, the European Economic and Social Committee and the Committee of the Regions: Towards a Comprehensive Climate Change Agreement in Copenhagen*, 2009, p. 2, http://eur-lex.europa.eu/LexUriServ/LexUriServ.do?uri=COM:2009:0039:FIN:EN:PDF.

6. F. Pearce, "Climate Pieces Start to Stack Up," *New Scientist* (July 18–24, 2009): 8–9.

7. The Pew Research Center for People and the Press, "Internet Overtakes Newspapers as News Outlet," December 23, 2008, http://people-press.org/report/479/internet-overtakes-newspapers-as-news-source.

8. Society of Professional Journalists, *Code of Ethics* (Indianapolis: Society of Professional Journalists, 1996), www.spj.org/pdf/ethicscode.pdf.

9. B. H. Bagdikian, *The New Media Monopoly* (Boston: Beacon, 2004).

10. R. K. Pachauri and A. Reisinger, eds., *Climate Change 2007 Synthesis Report*, Intragovernmental Panel on Climate Change Fourth Assessment Report (Geneva: IPCC, 2007).

11. A notable exception to this is the National Science Foundation's Course Curriculum and Laboratory Improvement Program, which provides tiers of support for educational project development. Awardees are first given funds to develop projects; a subset of those receive more money to scale them up; and a subset of those may receive a considerable amount of support to widely disseminate new curricula and ideas.

FIVE. THE NEEDS OF ENVIRONMENTALLY ACTIVE CITIZENS

1. D. W. Orr, *Earth In Mind: On Education, Environment, and the Human Prospect* (Washington, DC: Island Press, 1994), 112.

2. M. Gladwell, *The Tipping Point: How Little Things Can Make a Big Difference* (Boston: Little, Brown, 2000). The term *tipping point* has

become a source of confusion, because different disciplines often mean different things when they use it. In physics, it refers to the point at which something shifts from one stable state of equilibrium to another. In climatology and environmental science, it typically refers to "points of no return" either known or unknown, where shifts in previously stable states become drastic and irreversible. In sociology, a tipping point is the moment when something out of the ordinary becomes mainstream.

3. D. K. Perovich, J. A. Richter-Menge, K. F. Jones, and B. Light, "Sunlight, Water, and Ice: Extreme Arctic Sea Ice Melt During the Summer of 2007," *Geophysical Research Letter* 35 (2008): L11501.

4. T. Lauck, C. W. Clark, M. Mangel, and G. R. Munro, "Implementing the Precautionary Principle in Fisheries Management Through Marine Reserves," *Ecological Applications* 8, no. 1 (1998): S72–S78.

5. P. R. Ehrlich and A. H. Ehrlich, *One with Nineveh: Politics, Consumption, and the Human Future* (Washington, DC: Island Press, 2004), 132.

6. U.S. Department of Defense, "The Budget for Fiscal 2009," www .gpoaccess.gov/usbudget/fy09/pdf/budget/defense.pdf. W. T. Wheeler, "What Do the Pentagon's Numbers Really Mean?" Center for Defense Information, What's New, February 4, 2008, www.cdi.org/program/document.cfm?DocumentID=4199.

7. C. W. Clark, "Profit Maximization and the Extinction of Animal Species," *Journal of Political Economy* 81, no. 4 (1973): 950–961.

8. S. Amir, "Harvesting to Extinction: Is It Socially Rational?" *Journal of Bioeconomics* 4 (2002): 135–162.

9. D. Pauly, "Anecdotes and the Shifting Baselines Syndrome of Fisheries," *Trends in Ecology and Evolution* 10, no. 10 (1995): 430.

10. P. J. Crutzen and E. F. Stoermer, "The 'Anthropocene,'" *Global Change Newsletter* 41 (2000): 17–18.

11. G. Santayana, *The Life of Reason; or, the Phases of Human Progress* (New York: Charles Scribner's Sons, 1905).

12. L. Quaid, "Obama Offers 'Race to the Top' Contest for Schools," *The Guardian,* July 24, 2009.

SIX. BETWEEN AWARENESS AND ACTION

1. J. Swim, S. Clayton, T. Doherty, R. Gifford, G. Howard et al., *Psychology and Global Climate Change: Addressing a Multi-faceted Phenomenon and Set of Challenges* (Washington, DC: American Psychological Association, 2009), www.apa.org/releases/climate-change.pdf.

2. Campaign for Tobacco-Free Kids, *A Broken Promise to Our Children: The 1998 State Tobacco Settlement Eight Years Later* (Washington, DC: Campaign for Tobacco-Free Kids, December 6, 2006), www.tobaccofreekids.org/reports/settlements/2007/fullreport.pdf.

3. S. Khanna, "Q&A: The Science of Persuasion," *Nature* 461, no. 22 (2009): 1069.

4. D. Sobel, *Beyond Ecophobia: Reclaiming the Heart in Nature Education,* Orion Society Nature Literacy Series, vol. 1 (Great Barrington, MA: Orion Society, 1996).

5. K. Lisagor, "Bird-Watching Is Looking Up," Travel, *USA Weekend Magazine,* 2006, www.usaweekend.com/06_issues/060507/060507travelsmart.html.

6. A. Leopold, *A Sand County Almanac, and Sketches Here and There* (New York: Oxford University Press, 1949), 119.

7. P. A. Zaradic, O. R. W. Pergams, and P. Kareiva, "The Impact of Nature Experience on Willingness to Support Conservation," *Public Library of Science One* 4, no. 10 (2009): e7367, www.plosone.org/article/info:doi%2F10.1371%2Fjournal.pone.0007367.

8. O. R. W. Pergams and P. A. Zaradic, "Evidence for a Fundamental and Pervasive Shift Away From Nature-Based Recreation," *Proceedings of the National Academy of Sciences of the United States* 105, no. 7 (2008): 2295–2300, www.pnas.org/content/105/7/2295.full.pdf+html.

9. A. Balmford, J. Beresford, J. Green, R. Naidoo, M. Walpole, and A. Manica, "A Global Perspective on Trends in Nature-Based Tourism," *Public Library of Science—Biology* 7, no. 6 (2009): 1–6, www.plosbiology.org/article/info%3Adoi%2F10.1371%2Fjournal.pbio.1000144.

10. International Ecotourism Society, "Our Mission," n.d., www.ecotourism.org/site/c.orLQKXPCLmF/b.4835251/k.FF11/Our_Mission__The_International_Ecotourism_Society.htm.

11. J. A. Cousins, J. Evans, and J. Saddler, "Selling Conservation? Scientific Legitimacy and the Commodification of Conservation Tourism," *Ecology and Society* 14, no. 1 (2009): 32, www.ecologyandsociety.org/vol14/iss1/art32/.

12. D. Sobel, *Place-Based Education: Connecting Classrooms and Communities* (Great Barrington, MA: Orion Society, 2004).

13. Ibid., 59.

14. L. Mann and M. Coble, "A Little Salad Dressing Goes a Long Way," Program Profile, Environmental Education and Training Partnership, 2006, http://cms.eetap.org/repository/moderncms_documents/ALittleSaladDressingGoesALongWay.1.pdf.

15. Centers for Disease Control and Prevention, "Diabetes Data and Trends: Number (in Millions) of Civilian/Noninstitutionalized Persons with Diagnosed Diabetes, United States, 1980–2006," 2008, www.cdc.gov/diabetes/statistics/prev/national/figpersons.htm. C. L. Ogden, M. D. Carroll, L. R. Curtin, M. A. McDowell, C. J. Tabak, and J. M. Flegal, "Prevalence of Overweight and Obesity in the United States, 1999–2004," *Journal of the American Medical Association* 295, no. 13 (2006): 1549–1555.

SEVEN. A POLITICAL PRIMER

1. *The Federalist Papers: No. 39*, the Avalon Project, Documents in Law, History and Diplomacy, Yale Law School, Lillian Goldman Law Library, http://avalon.law.yale.edu/18th_century/fed39.asp.

2. "62% Hold Populist, or Mainstream, Views," Rasmussen Reports, September 18, 2009, www.rasmussenreports.com/public_content/politics/ideology/62_hold_populist_or_mainstream_views.

3. M. Barbaro, "Bloomberg Spent $102 Million to Win 3rd Term," *New York Times*, November 28, 2009, www.nytimes.com/2009/11/28/nyregion/28spending.html?_r=1.

4. The totals for the 2008 election cycle are based on Federal Election Commission data released electronically: "Campaign Finance Reports and Data," October 27, 2008, Federal Election Commission, www.fec.gov/disclosure.shtml.

5. World Bank, *World Development Report 1997: The State in a Changing World* (Oxford: Oxford University Press, 1997), 102.

6. Transparency International, *Global Corruption Report 2008: Corruption in the Water Sector* (Cambridge: Cambridge University Press, 2008), 297–302.

7. S. Winbourne, *Corruption and the Environment* (Washington, DC: USAID and Management Systems International, 2002), http://pdf.dec.org/pdf_docs/PNACT876.pdf. S. Morse, "Is Corruption Bad for Environmental Sustainability?: A Cross-National Analysis," *Ecology and Society* 11, no. 1 (2006): 22, www.ecologyandsociety.org/vol11/iss1/art22/.

8. J. Madison, "The Federalist No. 10: The Utility of the Union as a Safeguard Against Domestic Faction and Insurrection (continued)," *Daily Advertiser,* November 22, 1787, www.constitution.org/fed/federa10.htm.

9. Salary Wizard Basic Report, Salary.com, http://swz.salary.com/salarywizard/layouthtmls/swzl_compresult_national_CM02000070.html.

10. R. G. Kaiser, *So Damn Much Money: The Triumph of Lobbying and the Corrosion of American Government* (New York: Knopf, 2009), 7, 360, 340.

11. S. Schmidt and J. V. Grimaldi, "Abramoff Pleads Guilty to 3 Counts," *Washington Post,* January 4, 2006.

12. W. D. Hartung and M. Ciarrocca, *The Ties That Bind: Arms Industry Influence on the Bush Administration and Beyond* (New York: World Policy Institute, 2004), www.worldpolicy.org/projects/arms/reports/TiesThatBind.html.

13. R. Leung, "Cashing In for Profit?" CBS News.com, January 4, 2005, www.cbsnews.com/stories/2005/01/04/60II/main664652.shtml.

14. J. Tankersley and J. Meyer, "Former Interior Secretary Gale Norton Is Focus of Corruption Probe," *Los Angeles Times,* September 17, 2009, www.latimes.com/news/nationworld/nation/la-na-norton17-2009sep17,0,6215749.story. T. Capaccio, "Raytheon's Lynn Confirmed as Deputy Defense Secretary," Bloomberg.com, www.bloomberg.com/apps/news?pid=20601087&sid=ahdLvHNW4z.4&refer=home#.

15. J. Rood, "Despite Obama's Promises, Revolving Door Still Turning," ABC News.com, 2009, http://abcnews.go.com/Blotter/story?id=8296591&page=1&page=1.

16. E. Schmitt, "New Lobbying Rules, From Bagels to Caviar," *New York Times,* February 11, 1996, www.nytimes.com/1996/02/11/us/new-lobbying-rules-from-bagels-to-caviar.html?pagewanted=1.

17. "COP15 Copenhagen: The United Nations Climate Change Conference 2009," www.denmark.dk/en/menu/Climate-Energy/COP15-Copenhagen-2009/cop15.htm.

18. D. Goleman, *Ecological Intelligence: How Knowing the Hidden Impacts of What We Buy Can Change Everything* (New York: Broadway Books, 2009).

19. W. L. Lunch and P. W. Sperlich, "American Public Opinion and the War in Vietnam," *Western Political Quarterly* 32, no. 1 (1979): 26.

20. Lyndon B. Johnson, 388—the President's News Conference, July 28, 1965, the American Presidency Project, www.presidency.ucsb.edu/ws/index.php?pid=27116.

21. M. S. Molina and F. S. Rowland, "Stratospheric Sink for Chlorofluoromethanes: Chlorine Atom-Catalysed Destruction of Ozone," *Nature* 249 (1974): 810–812.

22. United Nations Environmental Programme, *The 1987 Montreal Protocol on Substances That Deplete the Ozone Layer (as agreed in 1987),* 1987, United Nations Environmental Programme, Ozone Secretariat, http://ozone.unep.org/Ratification_status/montreal_protocol.shtml.

23. United Nations Environmental Programme, "Evolution of the Montreal Protocol," 2009, United Nations Environmental Programme, Ozone Secretariat, http://ozone.unep.org/Ratification_status/.

24. P. R. Ehrlich and A. H. Ehrlich, *The Dominant Animal: Human Evolution and the Environment* (Washington, DC: Island Press, 2008).

25. Green Belt Movement, "What Is the Greenbelt Movement: A Vision Statement," http://greenbeltmovement.org/a.php?id=178.

26. "Letter from Wangari Maathai," n.d., Green Belt Movement, www.greenbeltmovement.org/w.php?id=58.

27. D. Michaels, *Doubt Is Their Product: How Industry's Assault on Science Threatens Your Health* (New York: Oxford University Press, 2008).

28. Hill & Knowlton, "Case Studies," n.d., www.hillandknowlton.com/casestudies.

29. Pew Research Center for the People and the Press, *Fewer Americans See Solid Evidence of Global Warming* (Washington, DC: Pew Research Center for the People and the Press, October 22, 2009), 2, http://people-press.org/report/?pageid=1604.

30. R. A. Kerr, "Amid Worrisome Signs of Warming, 'Climate Fatigue' Sets In," *Science* 136 (2009): 926–928.

EIGHT. CONSUMPTION, CONSERVATION, AND CHANGE

1. Environmental Literacy Council, "Cell Phone Life Cycle," 2002, www.enviroliteracy.org/article.php/1119.html.

2. N. H. Stern, *The Economics of Climate Change: The Stern Review* (Cambridge: Cambridge University Press, 2007).

3. J. E. Anderson, "A Conceptual Framework for Evaluating and Quantifying Naturalness," *Conservation Biology* 5 (1991): 347–352.

4. P. R. Ehrlich and J. P. Holdren, "Impact of Population Growth," *Science* 171 (1971): 1212–1217.

5. P. R. Ehrlich and J. P. Holdren, "A Bulletin Dialog—Critique," *Bulletin of the Atomic Scientists* 28, no. 5 (1972): 16, 18–27, http://books.google.com/books?id=pwsAAAAMBAJ&pg=PA1&source=gbs_toc_pages&cad=0_1#v=onepage&q=&f=false. B. Commoner, "On the Closing Circle—Response," *Bulletin of the Atomic Scientists* 28, no. 5 (1972): 17, 42–56, http://books.google.com/books?id=pwsAAAAMBAJ&pg=PA1&source=gbs_toc_pages&cad=0_1#v=onepage&q=&f=false.

6. P. E. Waggoner and J. H. Ausubel, "A Framework for Sustainability Science: A Renovated IPAT Identity," *Proceedings of the National Academy of Sciences* 99, no. 12 (2002): 7860.

7. R. York, E. A. Rosa, and T. Dietz, "STIRPAT, IPAT and ImPACT: Analytic Tools for Unpacking the Driving Forces of Environmental Impacts," *Ecological Economics* 46 (2003): 351–365.

8. T. Dietz, E. A. Rosa, and R. York, "Driving the Human Ecological Footprint," *Frontiers in Ecology and the Environment* 5, no. 1 (2007): 13–18.

9. R. Levins, "The Strategy of Model Building in Population Biology," *American Scientist* 54, no. 4 (1966): 421–431.

10. P. R. Ehrlich, *The Population Bomb* (New York: Ballantine, 1968).

11. World Resources Institute Earth Trends: The Environmental Information Portal, http://earthtrends.wri.org/searchable_db/index.php?theme=g&variable_id=351&action=select_countries.

12. United Nations Population Fund and Population Reference Bureau, *Country Profiles for Population and Reproductive Health: Policy Developments and Indicators 2005,* 2005, www.unfpa.org/upload/lib_pub_file/524_filename_country_profiles_2005.pdf.

13. U.S. Census Bureau, *Annual Estimates of the Resident Population for the United States, Regions, States, and Puerto Rico: Apri 1, 2000 to July 1, 2008,* NST-EST2008–01, 2009, www.census.gov/popest/states/NST-ann-est.html.

14. U.S. Department of Energy, "Energy Sources: Fossil Fuels," 2009, www.energy.gov/energysources/fossilfuels.htm.

15. Progressive Insurance X Prize Foundation, "Competition Guidelines: Version 1.2," January 13, 2009, www.progressiveautoxprize.org/files/downloads/auto/PIAXP_Guidelines_V_1.0_20090110.pdf.

16. U.S. Green Building Council, LEED Certification Program, www.usgbc.org/DisplayPage.aspx?CMSPageID=1988.

17. Natural Resources Defense Council, *Building Green: From Principle to Practice,* 2009, www.nrdc.org/buildinggreen/default.asp.

18. W. S. Jevons, *The Coal Question,* 1866, Library of Economics and Liberty, accessed December 13, 2009, www.econlib.org/library/YPDBooks/Jevons/jvnCQ0.html.

19. C. Raffensperger and J. Tickner, eds., *Protecting Public Health and the Environment* (Washington, DC: Island Press, 1999).

20. Lawrence Berkeley National Laboratory, Energy Analysis Department, "Standby Power," 2009, http://standby.lbl.gov/.

21. Blackle Internet Portal, home page, www.blackle.com/.

22. P.M. Rossett, *The Multiple Functions and Benefits of Small Farm Agriculture: In the Context of Global Trade Negotiations,* Policy Brief No. 4 (Oakland, CA: Institute for Food and Development Policy, 1999).

23. M. Specter, "Big Foot: In Measuring Carbon Emissions, It's Easy to Confuse Morality and Science," *New Yorker,* February 25, 2008, 44–53.

24. Alice E. Beetz, "A Brief Overview of Nutrient Cycling in Pastures," 2002, National Sustainable Agriculture Information Service, http://attra.ncat.org/attra-pub/summaries/nutcycle.html.

25. E. Stehfest, L. Bouwman, D. van Vuuren, M. den Elzen, B. Eickhout, and P. Kabat, "Climate Benefits of Changing Diet," *IOP Conference Series: Earth and Environmental Science* 6 (2009): 262009.

26. J. Giles, "Eating Less Meat Could Cut Climate Costs," *New Scientist* 14 (2009): 49.

27. J.H. Kunstler, *The Long Emergency: Surviving the Converging Catastrophes of the Twenty-First Century* (New York: Grove Press, 2006).

28. F. Pearce, *Confessions of an Eco-Sinner: Tracking Down the Sources of My Stuff* (Boston: Beacon Press, 2008).

29. World Commission on Environment and Development, *Our Common Future* (Oxford: Oxford University Press, 1987), 262.

30. G. Hardin, "The Tragedy of the Commons," *Science* 162, no. 3859 (1968): 1243–1248, www.sciencemag.org/cgi/content/full/162/3859/1243.

31. E. Ostrom, "The Challenge of Common-Pool Resources," *Environment Magazine,* July–August 2007, www.environmentmagazine.org/Archives/Back%20Issues/July-August%202008/ostrom-full.html.

32. A. Chhatre and A. Agrawal, "Trade-Offs and Synergies between Carbon Storage and Livelihood Benefits from Forest Commons," *Proceedings of the National Academy of Sciences* 106, no. 42 (October 20, 2009), www.pnas.org_cgi_doi_10.1073_pnas.0905308106.

33. Hardin, "Tragedy of the Commons," 1245.

NINE. AN EVOLVING METRIC

1. "Exercise and the Effects on Blood Pressure (BP)," General Practice Notebook, www.gpnotebook.co.uk/simplepage.cfm?ID= -1798307834&linkID=24246&cook=yes. "Efficacy of Reducing Blood Pressure with Salt Reduction," www.dashdiet.org.

2. G. V. Glass, "Meta-Analysis at 25," 2000, http://glass.ed.asu.edu/ gene/papers/meta25.html.

3. Collaboration for Environmental Evidence, "What Is Evidence-Based Conservation?" 2009, www.environmentalevidence.org/ EBConservation.htm.

4. "The Impacts of Expert Systems on Healthcare: Economic Considerations," University of Pittsburgh, www.pitt.edu/~super1/lecture/ lec5791/index.htm.

5. S. A. Nan, "Formative Evaluation," Beyond Intractability," 2003, www.beyondintractability.org/essay/formative_evaluation/. M. Scriven, *Evaluation Thesaurus* (Newberry Park, CA: Sage, 1991).

6. American Institutes for Research, *Effects of Outdoor Education Programs for Children in California,* 2005, www.tcoe.k12.ca.us/SCICON/ AB1330FinalReport.pdf.

7. M. Q. Patton, *How to Use Qualitative Methods in Evaluation* (Newberry Park, CA: Sage, 1987).

8. C. Price, "Five Frequently Asked Questions," *Renewal Magazine* (Association of Waldorf Schools of North America, New York) 12, no. 1 (2003).

9. S. H. Schneider, "A Better Way to Learn," *World Monitor,* April 1993, 35.

10. C. Wieman, "Why Not Try a Scientific Approach to Science Education?" *Change,* September–October 2007, www.changemag.org/ Archives/Back%20Issues/September-October%202007/index.html.

TEN. AND HOW WE CAN FIX IT

1. T. L. Friedman, "The Inflection Is Near?" *New York Times,* March 8, 2009, WK12, www.nytimes.com/2009/03/08/opinion/08friedman .html?_r=1.

2. J. Diamond, *Collapse: How Societies Choose to Fail or Succeed* (New York: Penguin, 2005).

3. California State Board of Education, *Science Content Standards* (Sacramento: California State Board of Education, 1998), www.cde .ca.gov/BE/ST/SS/documents/sciencestnd.pdf.

4. B. K. Rodes and R. Odell, *A Dictionary of Environmental Quotations* (Baltimore: Johns Hopkins University Press, 1997), 33.

5. North American Association for Environmental Education, *The Excellence in Environmental Education—Guidelines for Learning (Pre K–12) Executive Summary and Self Assessment Tool* (Washington, DC: NAAEE, 2004).

6. R. Hopkins, *The Transition Handbook: From Oil Dependency to Local Resilience* (White River Junction, VT: Chelsea Green, 2008).

7. L. Smith, "D.C. Schools Chief Michelle Rhee Fights Unions Over Teacher Pay," *U.S. News & World Report*, December 21, 2009, www. usnews.com/articles/news/national/2009/12/21/dc-schools-chief-michelle-rhee-fights-union-over-teacher-pay.html.

8. P. McGreevy and H. Blume, "Assembly OKs Bills to Change California Schools," *Los Angeles Times,* January 5, 2010, http://articles .latimes.com/2010/jan/05/local/la-me-schools6–2010jan06.

SELECTED BIBLIOGRAPHY

Allen, A. "Prodigal Sun." *Mother Jones,* March–April 2000, *www.motherjones .com/politics/2000/03/prodigal-sun.*

Ariely, D. *Predictably Irrational: The Hidden Forces That Shape Our Decisions.* New York: Harper, 2008.

Biello, D. "Another Inconvenient Truth: The World's Growing Population Poses a Malthusian Dilemma." *Scientific American,* October 2, 2009.

Blumstein, D. T. "Darwinian Decision-Making: Putting the Adaptive into Adaptive Management." *Conservation Biology* 21 (2007): 552–553.

Blumstein, D. T., and C. Saylan. "Essay: The Failure of Environmental Education (And How We Can Fix It)." *Public Library of Science—Biology* 5, no. 5 (2007): e120.

Carson, R. L. *Silent Spring.* Boston: Houghton Mifflin, 1962.

Carter, T. S. "The Failure of Environmental Regulation in New York." *Crime, Law and Social Change* 26, no. 1 (1996): 27–52.

Centre for Evidence-Based Conservation, www.cebc.bangor.ac.uk.

Child, M. F. "The Thoreau Ideal as a Unifying Thread in the Conservation Movement." *Conservation Biology* 23, no. 2 (2009): 241–243.

Commoner, B. *The Closing Circle.* New York: Random House, 1971.

CREEC Network. California Regional Environmental Education Community, www.creec.org/.

Daly, H. "Uneconomic Growth in Theory and Fact" (1999), in *FEASTA Review,* No. 1, ed. R. G. Douthwaite and J. Jopling (Dublin, Ireland: Green Books, 2001), www.feasta.org/documents/feastareview/daly.htm.

———. "Three Anathemas on Limiting Economic Growth." *Conservation Biology* 23, no. 2 (2009): 252–253.

Dewey, J. *Democracy and Education: An Introduction to the Philosophy of Education.* New York: Macmillan, 1916.

Diamond, J. *Collapse: How Societies Choose to Fail or Succeed.* New York: Penguin, 2005.

Dodds, W. K. *Humanity's Footprint: Momentum, Impact and Our Global Environment.* New York: Columbia University Press, 2008.

Ehrlich, P. R., and A. H. Ehrlich. *One with Nineveh: Politics, Consumption, and the Human Future.* Washington, DC: Island Press, 2004.

———. *The Dominant Animal: Human Evolution and the Environment.* Washington, DC: Island Press, 2008.

Ellis, R. *The Empty Ocean.* Washington, DC: Island Press/Shearwater Books, 2003.

Erikson, E. *Childhood and Society.* New York: W. W. Norton, 1950.

Freire, P. *Education for Critical Consciousness.* New York: Continuum, 2008.

Gintis, H., H. Bowles, R. Boyd, and E. Fehr. "Explaining Altruistic Behavior in Humans." *Evolution and Human Behavior* 24 (2003): 153–172.

Gladwell, M. *The Tipping Point: How Little Things Can Make a Big Difference.* Boston: Little, Brown, 2000.

Goleman, D. *Ecological Intelligence: How Knowing the Hidden Impacts of What We Buy Can Change Everything.* New York: Broadway Books, 2009.

Gore, A. *The Assault on Reason.* New York: Penguin, 2007.

Grifo, F., T. Donaghy, P. Baur, M. Halpern, K. Kaufman et al. *Federal Science and the Public Good: Securing the Integrity of Science in Policy Making.* Cambridge, MA: Union of Concerned Scientists, 2008.

Harte, J., and M. E. Harte. "Cool the Earth, Save the Economy: Solving the Climate Crisis Is EASY," 2008, http://cooltheearth.us/download.php.

Hawken, P. *Blessed Unrest: How the Largest Social Movement in History Is Restoring Grace, Justice, and Beauty to the World.* New York: Penguin, 2007.

Hayes, M. A. "Into the Field: Naturalistic Education and the Future of Conservation." *Conservation Biology* 23, no. 5 (2009): 1075–1079.

Helvarg, D. *The War Against the Greens.* San Francisco: Sierra Club Books, 1994.

Hickman, L. A., and T. M. Alexander, eds. *The Essential Dewey: Pragmatism, Education, Democracy.* Vol. 1. Bloomington: Indiana University Press, 1998.

Hopkins, R. *The Transition Handbook: From Oil Dependency to Local Resilience.* White River Junction, VT: Chelsea Green, 2008.

Huxley, A. *Brave New World.* London: Chatto and Windus, 1932.

Kaiser, R. G. *So Damn Much Money: The Triumph of Lobbying and the Corrosion of American Government.* New York: Knopf, 2009.

Kaufman, W. *No Turning Back: Dismantling the Fantasies of Environmental Thinking.* New York: Basic Books, 1994.

Keene, M., and D. T. Blumstein. "Environmental Education: A Time of Change, a Time for Change." *Journal of Evaluation and Program Planning* 33 (2010): 201–204.

Kunstler, J. H. *The Long Emergency: Surviving the Converging Catastrophes of the Twenty-First Century.* New York: Grove Press, 2006.

Leopold, A. *A Sand County Almanac, and Sketches Here and There.* New York: Oxford University Press, 1949.

Levin, S. A. *Fragile Dominion: Complexity and the Commons.* Reading, MA: Helix Books, 1999.

Louv, R. *Last Child in the Woods: Saving Our Children From Nature-Deficit Disorder.* Chapel Hill, NC: Algonquin Books, 2008.

Lovelock, J. *The Vanishing Face of Gaia: A Final Warning.* New York: Basic Books, 2009.

Maathai, W. *The Green Belt Movement: Sharing the Approach and the Experience.* New York: Lantern Books, 2006.

Madison, J. *James Madison: Writings.* New York: Library of America, 1999.

McKibben, B. *The End of Nature.* New York: Random House, 2006.

McLaren, P. *Life in Schools: An Introduction to Critical Pedagogy in the Foundations of Education.* Boston: Allyn and Bacon, 2003.

Michaels, D. *Doubt Is Their Product: How Industry's Assault on Science Threatens Your Health.* New York: Oxford University Press, 2008.

Miller, P. Energy Conservation: It Starts at Home. *National Geographic,* March 2009, http://ngm.nationalgeographic.com/2009/03/energy-conservation/miller-text/1.

Montesquieu, Charles de Secondat, baron de. *Selected Political Writings*. Indianapolis: Hackett, 1990.

Mora, C., R. A. Myers, M. Coll, S. Libralato, T. J. Pitcher et al. "Management Effectiveness of the World's Marine Fisheries." *Public Library of Science— Biology* 7, no. 6 (2009): e1000131.

Morrisette, P. M. "The Evolution of Policy Responses to Stratospheric Ozone Depletion." *Natural Resources Journal* 29 (1989): 793–820.

Moyers, B. *Moyers On Democracy*. New York: Doubleday, 2008.

Muir, J. *John Muir: Nature Writings*. New York: Library of America, 1997.

Nestle, M. *What to Eat*. New York: North Point Press, 2006.

———. *Food Politics: How the Food Industry Influences Nutrition and Health*. 2nd ed. Berkeley: University of California Press, 2007.

Office of Management and Budget. "Rating the Performance of Federal Programs," 2004, www.whitehouse.gov/omb/rewrite/budget/fy2004/ performance.html.

Orr, D. W. *Earth in Mind: On Education, Environment, and the Human Prospect*. Washington, DC: Island Press, 1994.

———. *Down to the Wire: Confronting Climate Collapse*. New York: Oxford University Press, 2009.

———. "The New Design Revolution." *Center for Ecoliteracy: Writings Online*, 2009, www.ecoliteracy.org/publications/david_orr_design_revolution .html.

Participant Media. *Food, Inc. Discussion Guide*. Berkeley, CA: Center for Ecoliteracy, 2009, www.ecoliteracy.org/publications/food_inc.html.

Pearce, F. *Confessions of an Eco-Sinner: Tracking Down the Sources of My Stuff*. Boston: Beacon, 2008.

———. "Let the People Look After Their Forests." *New Scientist* 24, no. 2729 (2009).

Pew Center on Global Climate Change. "Climate Change 101: Understanding and Responding to Global Climate Change," 2009, www.pewclimate .org/global-warming-basics/climate_change_101.

Piaget, J., and B. Inhelder. *The Psychology of the Child*. New York: Basic Books, 1969.

Pimm, S. L. *World According to Pimm*. New York: McGraw-Hill, 2001.

Pollan, M. *An Omnivore's Dilemma: A Natural History of Four Meals.* New York: Penguin, 2006.

Postman, N. *Building a Bridge to the Eighteenth Century.* New York: Alfred A. Knopf, 1999.

Rousseau, J.J. *The Social Contract.* Chicago: Gateway Edition, 1954.

Shabecoff, P. *A New Name for Peace: International Environmentalism, Sustainable Development, and Democracy.* Hanover, NH: University Press of New England, 1996.

Sobel, D. *Beyond Ecophobia: Reclaiming the Heart in Nature Education.* Orion Society Nature Literacy Series, vol. 1. Great Barrington, MA: Orion Society, 1996.

————. *Place-Based Education: Connecting Classrooms and Communities.* Great Barrington, MA: Orion Society, 2004.

————. *Childhood and Nature: Design Principles for Educators.* Portland, ME: Stenhouse, 2008.

Starrs, T. "Fossil Food: Consuming Our Future." Center for Ecoliteracy, 2009, www.ecoliteracy.org/publications/rsl/tom-starrs.html.

Stone, M.K. *Smart By Nature: Schooling for Sustainability.* Healdsburg, CA: Watershed Media, 2009.

Thoreau, H.D. *Walden and Other Writings.* New York: Random House, 2000.

Tocqueville, A. de. *Democracy in America.* New York: Signet Classic, 2001.

Vygotsky, L.S. *Mind in Society: The Development of Higher Psychological Processes.* Cambridge, MA: Harvard University Press, 1978.

————. *Thought and Language.* Cambridge, MA: MIT Press, 1986.

Weigl, P.D. "The Natural History Conundrum Revisited: Mammalogy Begins at Home." *Journal of Mammalogy* 90, no. 2 (2009): 265–269.

Wilson, E.O. *The Creation: An Appeal to Save Life on Earth.* New York: W.W. Norton, 2006.

Zinn, H. *A Power Governments Cannot Suppress.* San Francisco: City Lights Books, 2007.

Zint, M., and N. Montgomery. "Welcome to MEERA." 2008. MEERA: My Environmental Education Evaluation Resource Assistant, http://meera.snre.umich.edu.

ACKNOWLEDGMENTS

The authors thank Hannah Love, Lynn Meinhardt, Heather Vaughan, Jacqueline Volin, and Jenny Wapner at University of California Press for their help and guidance. We thank Bonita Hurd for her diligent and clearheaded editing of the manuscript. We also thank Liza Gross for helping us publish our initial essay, and Patrick Fitzgerald for encouraging us to transform that vision into a book.

Charlie: I thank my wife, Maddalena Bearzi, for her unwavering love, support, and patience, not just in the realization of this book, of which she was an integral part, but also in life, which she brightens daily. I also thank my aunt and friend Marcelyn Saylan for her love and support and her many pertinent insights gained over her career as a LAUSD teacher and school psychologist. I thank my friends Paul Berger, Joanna Arluckiewicz, Carin Bokhof, and Michael Navarro for their valuable thoughts and comments, as well as for the many hours spent listening to my ramblings on environmental education. Finally, I thank the research volunteers and supporters of Ocean Conservation Society for providing me with the opportunity to work toward a better world.

Dan: I thank Ken Armitage, Kevin Armitage, Dave Armstrong, Billy Barr, Maddalena Bearzi, Marc Bekoff, Ian Billick, Paul and Anne Ehrlich, Esteban Fernández-Juricic, Johannes Foufopolous, John and Mel Harte, David and Bonnie Inouye, Matt Keene, Devra Kleiman, Cully Nordby, David Orr, Tom Smith, Bill Sutherland, and Eugene Volokh for advice, stimulating discussions, and inspiration about environmental education, conservation, and evaluation. My parents have been influential in cultivating my love for nature. I thank my father, Ed Blumstein, for introducing me to nature and natural places, and my mother, Sandra Agrons, for that first memorable Earth Day experience, through which we both learned that polluted water can be clear. My wife, best friend, and colleague, Janice Daniel, has been a constant sounding board for all things educational, as well as a great partner for exploring all things environmental. We both hope that our son, David, has the opportunities we had, and we both work hard to make it so; this book is part of that effort. Over the years, my research has been supported by a Fulbright Fellowship, the American Institute for Pakistan Studies, the National Institute of Health, the National Science Foundation, the Australian Research Foundation, the National Geographic Society, and the University of California (Davis and Los Angeles), and I am grateful to my sponsors for giving me a first-class environmental education. I am particularly grateful to my academic homes—the Department of Ecology and Evolutionary Biology and the Institute of the Environment and Sustainability at UCLA—for creating a wonderful atmosphere for scholarship and discovery. Finally, I thank the Rocky Mountain Biological Laboratory, the high-alpine field station in Gothic, Colorado, that is my summer base, for creating a stimulating intellectual atmosphere conducive to learning about the intersection between science, education, and policy.

INDEX

Abramoff, Jack, 121
academic tenure, 192–193
accountability: in education,
26, 166, 196; institutional
mind-set and, 66. *See also*
responsibility
acidification, of oceans, 12–13
action, 95–96, 115, 175–176; denial
and inaction, 38–39, 44–45, 97,
151, 174; educating to inspire, 28,
31, 32, 45, 47–48, 50–51, 109–110;
institutional mind-set and, 61,
71; international efforts, 60–61,
126, 130, 141–142, 154–157; making sacrifices, 176–177; models of
success, 51–52, 127–132; political,
involving students in, 188–189;
political awareness and, 127, 132,
134; psychological barriers to,
55, 97–100. *See also* behavioral
changes; conservation; curriculum implementation; grassroots
action

adaptive management, 45–46,
162–163
advertising, 136–137, 154; crying
Indian commercial, 88
advocacy, in education, 28, 31
affluence. *See* wealth
agriculture, 11–12, 14, 141, 149–151. *See
also* food security
air conditioning, 42
alternative energy. *See* renewable
energy
American Clean Energy and Security Act, 58–59, 60, 62–63
American Clean Energy Jobs and
Power Act, 58, 59, 60
American Psychological Association, 97
Anderson, Jay, 138
anthropocentrism, 21–22, 44–45
antismoking campaigns, 98
art, 56, 186
The Assault on Reason (Gore), 118–119
athletics, 189

Text:	10.75/15 Janson
Display:	Janson
Indexer:	Thérèse Shere
Compositor:	Toppan Best-set Premedia Limited
Printer and binder:	Maple-Vail Book Manufacturing Group